A BOUQUET OF RANDOM THOUGHTS

Conversations with myself

BILL K KOUL

Vitasta

We connected nonstop with the world out there but remained disconnected with ourselves. We reached out to the stars but uprooted ourselves. We satisfied our senses but starved our soul. We befriended others but not ourselves. We existed more but lived less.

You can never be lonely when you are alone. When you are alone, you have the best opportunity to enjoy your own company and energise yourself from an infinite source of universal energy, as you are close to Nature. But when you are disconnected from yourself, you feel lonely and Nature stops nourishing you.

Well-lived moments define the essence and flavour of a well-lived life. Sadly, due to our material tendency to think and plan big days, which are few and far-between, most lives pass unloved and unused, without good memories. Most people lose the opportunity to live while they exist. The quality of life magnifies significantly if the smaller units of time–moments and minutes–are lived as beautifully and meaningfully as the larger units of time—hours and days.

Contents

Acknowledgement

This book, *A Bouquet of Random Thoughts*, is for all times. It is about life and the human nature. Open any page of this bouquet and pick up any thought. It covers themes pertaining to life, in the form of articles, passages, one-liners, poems and illustrations.

Words may be chosen by authors and philosophers but the messages originate from the one infinite ocean of knowledge and the truth. I acknowledge life for grinding me down and weathering me out, just as a stone is humbled and rounded off. Life squeezed me in several ways, similar to how a juicy fruit is squeezed by a hand. I felt bruised and battered, and my thoughts oozed incessantly, as life unfolded. Life has its unique ways of expressing itself. I had no control, whatsoever, on the designs and the processes of life. This book is based on my conversations with myself. Most of the thoughts penned in this book have universal themes, to a smaller or greater extent. Its contents are not intended to challenge or criticise any one person or any organisation or community in particular.

The book is inspired by Saadi Shirazi (Abu-Muhammad Muslim al-Din bin Abdallah Shirazi, 1210-1291), a great Persian philosopher and poet. Saadi starts his epic work, *Gulistan*, with the following words:

Of what use will be a dish of roses to thee?
Take a leaf from my rose-garden.
A flower endures but five or six days
But this rose-garden is always delightful.

Understandably, by rose-garden, Saadi would have meant *Gulistan.* I wish to show my deep indebtedness to my parents, elders, teachers and philosophers who have chiselled and shaped my thoughts. I must pay my humble homage to the 9th Sikh Guru, Guru Teg Bahadur Ji (1 April 1621- 24 November 1675) for his selfless sacrificial role in the history of India and Kashmiri Pandits. My wholehearted thanks to Bala Sahib Thackeray (23 January 1926-17 November 2012) for his benevolence and support to the exiled Pandits of Kashmir, without which they would not have reclaimed their lives during and after 1990. In the same spirit, I also wish to sincerely thank the people of Jammu for their benevolence, acceptance and tolerance for accommodating and rehabilitation of a major portion of the exiled Kashmiri Pandits community in Jammu after their exodus from Kashmir in January 1990.

Sincere thanks to my wife, Prof Dr Rekha Bhan Koul, for her support and putting up with me through my writing journey. This book would not have been complete without a significant input from my friend, Dr Farzad Beygi, for formatting and proofreading this book, and his intelligent, wise wife, Shadi Shahgaldi, for conceiving and drawing a series of thoughtful illustrations in this book.

Last, but not the least, my sincere thanks to Ms Renu Kaul Verma of Vitasta Publishing, New Delhi, for publishing this book and my editor, Ms Veena Batra, for her fine editing work and that too within a very short time frame.

Bill K Koul

Perth, Western Australia

Why Do I Write?

'Why do I write? Am I unwisely opinionated? Should I keep making noise?' I keep asking myself. From time to time, my independent thoughts may possibly be annoying some people when I don't tag along and feed their popular thoughts. In the current polarised world, many people will perceive me as a pseudo-intellectual or a pseudo-secular person because I don't jump aboard their bandwagon.

Something deep inside tells me to keep trying to make a positive difference in the world. I write for the people and their coming generations who can't speak for themselves at this point of time. In essence, knowingly or unknowingly, I may be leaving a legacy behind. On a conscious level though, I am preparing myself for the day of my reckoning when I will face myself. I do not want to feel small when I will ask myself in those final moments of my life, '*You could have done it, and did you even try? Why did you not play your part at least? You also turned out to be like most of them—an impotent, selfish coward.*'

There are times when I get tempted to resign from an uncontrollable urge to raise issues—tempted to accept what Nature has in destiny for India and its people—not in a much dissimilar way as most Indians have done. Like most others, then, should I resign and go about my life? Should I also believe in '*khao piyo mauj karo*'—the mantra for life and living in India—and follow the '*mainu kee*' attitude of most people? But that is not what the *Bhagwad Gita* says. Lord Krishna knew what would befall the *Kauravas*; in fact, he revealed it to *Arjuna*. But, at any stage, did he stop trying to avoid the war of the *Mahabharata*? No, he tried his level best to avoid the war. Sadly, the *Kauravas* chose the path of war and potential death.

I am not a policy-maker, nor am I a lawmaker. But, as a son of the soil, it is my responsibility to send a message—a constant message and constant reminders—to all those who have the authority and the means to implement the necessary changes which I am calling for. If I were at the helm, I would try to do the necessary. I am *nobody* in a relative sense. So, practically, all I can do is keep trying to be a voice of the helpless people and the future generations.

Despite the potential personal risks, occasional criticism and some discouragement, I keep trying hard. Many friends warn me, albeit in good faith, against attracting any undue attention of powerful people who benefit from disorder and issues. No wonder, not many people respond to my regular blogs, although verbally everyone compliments me in private, '*Nice, you write well. You target the issues head-on.*' I ask them, '*If that is the case, why do you people not respond to my blogs in public and join me in my campaign*?' A possible explanation is that not many people want to be identified on the public forum. Also, many people don't even have any opinion; they just follow one wave after the other, like herd. Once I asked two well-educated gentlemen if I should stop making noise. One of them said he would respond to my question during the day, but he never did; and the other gentleman did not even bother to respond.

Am I writing to change the people of the country? Yes and no, perhaps both. I do try to make a positive noise, with a strong hope that someone will hear my wailing cries and join me, and help me in drawing the attention of powerful stakeholders, who may help to implement the necessary measures to save the nation. I believe the time has come when India must face itself—is it one country or several? Religions—any for that matter—must not be allowed to define the national policies—otherwise further divisions are imminent.

Over the last three years or so, I have been relentlessly writing about India's issues in my books and blogs. But lately, I have been also experiencing an uncanny feeling that I may just be wasting my time—it may all be falling on deaf ears. People are not interested in reading about issues or worry about their solution; they live these issues every day in India and may have accepted them as a way of life and, therefore, virtually given up any hope that things will ever change for the better.

People are made to believe that it is impossible for anyone to turn things around. In fact, the (chaotic) pace of the everyday life in India, and the influence of social media, in tandem with the print and electronic media, does not allow people to think independently. As a result, many people are polarised and some have started believing in miracles. It is sad to see that, in general, the topics of discussion in India revolve around the people and personalities—politicians, actors, sports-persons, media bigwigs, history and historical figures—but not around real existential issues that undermine the country. For political correctness, and perhaps their personal safety, many people camouflage their thoughts.

I write on issues that confront India and the human life in general. One can't ignore a number of those serious issues—population growth, liveability, corruption, Kashmir, environment, human issues and education—that endanger India's sustainability and the human wellness. If being honest is a crime, then I shall continue to commit this crime. I am accountable to people. Let history judge me.

Take cover when dark clouds of the time look threatening

Rainbow is seen by those who dare to brave the rain

ONE

THE REALITY OF LIFE

Truth and Unhappiness Don't Go Together

AT HER CREMATION, he whispered, "Mother, I'll join you soon on the other side. I pray you find peace at last." It felt like one of their earlier parting hugs at the airport and railway station. As usual, his eyes were wet. But on this occasion, his hands shivered; they had just consigned her mortal remains to flames and he could never see her again. He felt uprooted, he had to support himself. His legs felt lifeless, they had to be dragged. His head felt heavy like lead and needed support but he did not see any shoulder to lean on. She had no siblings to lean on and share his memories of her.

About nine months earlier, he had been deeply concerned about her deteriorating health although she was relatively young, in her early sixties. He could tell that she was not quite well. He had cautioned his father about it. Accordingly, he had come and got her medically checked, over several days, at a famous private hospital, but doctors had not found anything overly concerning about her health.

Three months later, she was injured in a road accident. Her long scarf (*dupatta*), which was around her neck, was caught in the wheel of a cycle rickshaw that she was travelling on. She had momentarily passed out at that time and her gold chain had injured her neck. She had been rushed to the same famous hospital and luckily she revived. On learning about her accident a few days later, he flew immediately from overseas to see her. She looked a little weaker than her usual self.

A couple of months later, at a hill resort, where his parents had been holidaying away from the humidity of the plains, she had woken up one night with terrible backache. Also, she could not swallow her food easily. His father requested him to urgently fly home; he sounded desperate and helpless. None of his close relatives, who would holiday at his home a few times a year, had visited her or offered any help to his father.

On his arrival, after travelling about 12,000 km from the other side of the Equator, Chhotu, their faithful domestic helper, was surprised to see him. "Where are they?" he asked Chhottu, without exchanging any detailed greetings. "Upstairs, in their bedroom, bhaiya," replied Chhotu. He quickly ran upstairs. Their bedroom door was open. She was lying down on her bed, on her right side, moaning with pain. His father sat by her side, on a rug on the floor, seemingly clueless about the reason behind her pain and how to help her.

On seeing him, his father suddenly beamed with happiness; he stood up to greet him. But she could not sit up. She just looked at him and her eyes reflected love. He stood by her side and demanded her hug but she could not.

She kept moaning and painfully uttered, "This pain will kill me." His father announced, "She is not eating anything, she is being difficult. Her tests have come back normal. Perhaps, she has some psychological issues." Within the next couple of hours, a popular psychiatrist examined her at home and confirmed she was a very strong-willed person.

Early next morning, after his regular morning meditation, he ran 8 km on a dirt road in a neighbouring residential area. Running helped him to face difficult situations. He feared the worst now; he had feared it for the last couple of years. She was definitely not well.

During the day, he and his father met a popular orthopaedic specialist who advised an urgent CT scan on her. As she could not sit without experiencing extreme pain, it was a great chore to carry her to the clinic even after injecting her with a strong pain-killer. Two days later, the results confirmed the bad news. His world suddenly turned upside down and collapsed. He wondered: "How did this all happen? Why had no doctor earlier warned them about it? Why her? She is so young." He did not cry in front of his father.

On their way home in their car, he and his father promised each other to act normal at home till she was checked further by a specialist. She loved life; she did not want to die. Terminal diseases (in others) distressed her significantly. On reaching home, his mother asked, "How are the results? What did the doctor say?" "All good, please don't worry," replied his father, but he kept quiet.

After running upstairs, behind closed doors, he hit a bathroom wall several times with his fist and cried incessantly for several minutes. After filling himself with some faint hope for a miraculous medical cure, he washed his face and joined his father downstairs for lunch. *A drowning man catches at a straw*, as a saying goes. In a secret consultation with his father, they decided to fly her interstate at the earliest possible to consult specialists. As he did not have much cash with him, he borrowed some money from a close relative and some from a friend. Both lenders were benevolent and forthcoming.

Next day, they flew interstate and headed straight to a pre-organised, two-room, rented accommodation located near a specialised hospital, organised at a short notice by a well-wishing relative, who was sworn to extreme confidentiality. But flying her had proven to be a significant challenge. She had to be injected with a double dose of a strong pain-killer and made to lie down in the plane. Chhotu had also flown with them to help.

Over the next three days, he ran at a nearby park, setting himself stiffer challenges each day running more distance, over more time, making it more difficult for himself to run on those hot and humid days—wishing for a miracle. he had heard about Mughal Emperor Babar, who had (anecdotally) offered his own life for saving the life of his sick son, Humayun.

At the hospital, the doctors did all necessary tests on her, which confirmed the worst. He asked the specialist, "How long?"

"A maximum of six months," was the reply.

Nothing could be done to save her and it was only a matter of time. All they could do was to take her home and keep her as comfortable as possible. Although she was extraordinarily sharp, he and his father—by some Divine intervention—managed to keep a calm exterior to avoid raising any suspicion. He did not want her to die of shock before her biological death.

In confidence with his father, he decided to return home overseas at the earliest possible so that she did not become suspicious about her terminal illness. He promised her that he would return home in another two months, hoping the specialist's prediction (of 6 months) proved correct. The next evening he bid her goodbye. On the way to the airport and, thereafter, aboard those two long flights, he cried.

Over the next four weeks, he ran every day, steadily increasing his challenge with each day; he wished for a miracle. He would speak to his parents every day. She was a keen sports and political enthusiast. Once she said to him that she supported his national team against her national team, an expression of her motherly love. She also asked him to buy a digital camera, as a gift, for the compounder who injected her daily with a painkiller. He bought the camera within an hour of her request.

Exactly a month after his return, she passed on. As a miracle, he managed to reach home in time, within about 20 hours, to undertake her last rites. A few days after her cremation, he presented the camera to the compounder despite the latter's reluctance.

The decision to tell her the truth, or not, hinged on the possible outcome of the revelation. If the news could heal her or make her feel better, such truth was worth utterance. But in this case, given her nature, the truth would have shocked her and suddenly evaporated all her hopes and dreams of living a normal life. Hope sustains life. She had lived till her very end.

Reportedly, she had suffered a heart attack while watching

a television show. She had breathed her last in her husband's lap. She was just 63. To the extent he and his father knew, she did not know about the terminal nature of her illness. But as she was very intelligent, she may have possibly known it all along. What a family! Each one of them suffered internally but chose to live a normal life till her last breath. They never cried in public.

He[1] ran every morning during the mourning days. Although many people visited his home from far and wide for offering condolences, he felt very alone. On the morning of the 12th day ritual, during his morning run on the dirt track near his home, he overheard two elderly gentlemen from his community—completely unknown to him—chatting loudly. One of them said, "Yes, this is Kalyug. I have heard their only son lives overseas and does not care for them." But what did he know?

> *A truth is as good as the noble objective it serves. Any truth that has the potential to bring grief and suffering to anyone is better not uttered. Instead a lie that serves to bring joy and happiness to all is sweeter than the truth that brings sorrow. Adults tell so many fairy-tales to their children, which are all lies.*
>
> *Life is living one day at a time. Live it meaningfully. You never know if you will make it to the end of the day and then wake up the next morning.*
>
> *Your best friends and worst enemies are you yourself and the people you love the most.*
>
> *Your best friend and your worst enemy are closest to you. Choose carefully. Befriend one and unfriend one.*
>
> *You are alive till you are breathing and your heart is beating. Both these processes happen independent of your conscious*

1 The author

control or command. Before one or both these activities stop, take some time daily to observe them consciously and appreciate the miracle that your parents have created.

Mother Goddess

He was a handsome good-looking young man, a dentist by profession and a keen photographer, much ahead of his time and contrastingly different from all his relatives and peers. He was a philatelist and had a great collection of rare stamps from all over the world, which he prized in several albums. He was also a master at chess, carom and many other board games. He knew origami too. He wore white shoes—of different styles—and walked with an upright, distinct and dignified gait. He looked distinguished. In the summer months of Kashmir, he wore only white, cream or light lemon bush-shirts and crisp white or cream trousers.

In his breakfast, his mother would feed him a large glass of cow's milk, mixed with two raw eggs. Although, he did not like the taste of this cocktail, he drank it in complete obedience to his loving mother. He knew she had singlehandedly toiled extremely hard to keep him healthy since he had fallen extremely sick in his childhood. He owed his life to her, not once but on numerous occasions, and was deeply grateful to her. She was widowed in her early fifties. She had lost her husband at a very young age. Her personal income came from her late husband's pension.

Every morning, before leaving for work, he would bend down religiously and touch both her feet with his right hand, one after the other, and then touch both his eyes, one after the other, with the same hand. She was his deity; she had infused life into him time and again. She would keep her right hand on his head and utter her blessing, *"May God bless you with good health and keep you safe. May Mother Saraswati sit on your forehead and give your wisdom."* Then he would stand up, look at his mother with extreme gratitude, turn around, and pick up his office bag and leave. She would continue to stand there for a minute or two and keep uttering endless blessings for him, with moist eyes. This ritual between the two of them happened every day. Such a ritual, especially touching one's mother's feet, was rather uncommon in Kashmir. Thereafter, she would go inside her house, switch on her radio and listen to Kashmiri folk songs whilst sipping at her Kashmiri *sheer-chai* (pink, salted tea), and eat a local baker's bread. She was a good singer. She sang local folk songs with a sad but rich voice, reflecting deep pain in her heart.

She was a beautiful woman, affectionate and warm-hearted. She wore only white cotton saris, both in summer and winter of Kashmir. She was very fair, almost white, and her white hair matched her skin and sari. When she wore a red *teeka* (*bindi*) on her forehead, it stood out and she looked like a goddess. She was also an exceptionally good cook. With little resources sometimes, she could create lavish meal. Once, when it had snowed heavily and all shops were closed, she cooked seven different tasty dishes just out of potatoes for her grandson (the author) who was visiting her during his winter school holidays. She was a brave and strong woman——tenacious, resilient, beautiful, graceful, proud, wise, upright and loving. My grandmother was indeed a beautiful reflection of mother goddess.

It is true that, in essence, I am 'nothing' just a handful of dust, destined to go back to dust one day; or a tiny bubble, formed by a delicate film of ego of being, destined to burst suddenly some moment. It is only love that makes something of the nothing; otherwise life does not make any sense, whatsoever, at all.

Love gives a meaning and some dimension to life. It is love that keeps life going, one moment at a time—one breath at a time. No one knows the timing of that last one breath, which could be just a breath away. Live all moments fleeting by with love till that last one moment arrives. The invisible is destined to merge back with the invisible.

Love Conquers All

Vaali's unconditional love finally won me over. Vaali (named after Bali, the legendary Vanar king from the Ramayana) is a cute, 4-year old, Swiss Shepherd, with long snow-white fur and large dark black eyes. He was born to his pedigree parents and adopted as a 30-day old pup by my son. About two years ago, he moved interstate with with his adopted father (my son) when he moved with his job.

When Vaali joined our family three years ago, Sakha—our Siberian husky—was about 5 years old and the darling of the family. I was a little prejudiced in favour of Sakha, mainly because he conducted himself in a more mature and majestic manner, as a true alpha. In comparison, Vaali was relatively much more childlike, a little noisy and attention-seeking. I unfairly compared him with Sakha, forgetting he was just a pup. I had lost the wisdom that *one must appreciate everyone and never compare.*

Three days ago, Vaali saw me after a gap of nearly two years. He greeted me with such warmth that no words can describe. He looked very excited and kept leaping up for a long time to kiss and hug me. In his excitement, he also vomited and hardly ate anything over the next 24 hours. Over those two days, he followed me everywhere, even opened the bathroom door to look for me. He communicated through his eyes, distinct facial expressions and the vigorous movement of his long furry tail. He just could not—and perhaps never even tried—to hide his excitement; his tail gave away his feelings. Perhaps, he knew that I had earlier been a little prejudiced against him and was probably trying to win me over.

On the evening before I left his home, he looked sad and suddenly stopped interacting. His eyes reflected his sadness. Once, when he was napping with his head in my lap, he woke up and looked into my eyes with his large, sad eyes. Then he stood up and walked away to lie down near the door before sighing loudly. On the morning of my departure, he entered my bedroom and happily climbed on to my bed when I called him. He lay down silently beside me, while I patted him for a few minutes. It seemed to be a parting hug. He finally won me over. Pure, unconditional love always prevails.

There are several reasons why a dog is known to be a man's best friend and considered to be God's gift to man. Unlike humans, it loves unconditionally and just can't hide its emotions. By living in the moment, it teaches us how to live. It has much stronger senses of smell and hearing than humans and has the ability to see through them. We humans also breed, eat and relieve ourselves the same way as our dogs and cats, as sheep, cows and horses etc. But we must also learn from them about fairness and peaceful nature.

The human greed has no limits. We humans are also animals, but at the lower end of the spectrum of the animal kingdom. The brave amongst us are given the titles of 'lion', 'cheetah' and 'tiger'.

> *In terms of ethics, animals are much higher than humans. Animals are not greedy and conniving as we are; they kill and eat only when they are hungry.*
>
> *We humans are the most dangerous animals on the planet. We have made all kinds of weapons of mass destruction. We have ruined the environment. We gobble up the natural resources. We kill our own kind.*

Missed Opportunities, Time Waits for None

It so happens many a time in our lives when time is of the essence that we are caught napping in situations where we ought to have proactively lent a helping hand, in a timely manner. Time and tide do not wait for anyone. On such numerous occasions, my consciousness has tormented me time and again with niggling thoughts: I should have and I could have, but why didn't I? Why did I get frozen? Why did I miss the opportunity to help? I could have saved a life and several lives. Shame on me!

It has always been too late, too little. For example, I could have saved that little bird from getting crushed under the tyres of another car. Despite having the intent to, I did not save it. I was slow in my decision-making. So, I have blood on my hands, shame on me!

The story goes like this: I saw a little bird sitting paralysed in the middle of the road; the road traffic was much lower than the normal traffic due to school holidays. Despite feeling a little intoxicated due to lilting music playing on my car radio, I was alert enough to spot the little bird from a distance.

For a few seconds, I hoped the bird would fly away on hearing the sound of my car, just as birds usually do. But, when it did not shy away, I slowed down and carefully steered to the left and stopped my car in the exit lane, with the engine running. I was caught up in two minds: Should I drive away or should I pick up the bird and carry it to safety on the grassed kerbside? While I was still thinking, I was horrified to see a car in my rear mirror, fast approaching the bird in the same lane. Upon that, with deep remorse and anguish, I realised it was too late for me to disembark and undertake any rescue act. I prayed the driver of the approaching car spots the bird and changes lane. But, alas, that did not happen! The car ran past me, throwing a heap of white feathers in the air behind it. The poor bird was gone. I was just not quick enough in my decision-making. I felt deeply sad, inadequate and miserable.

In hindsight, I feel I could have saved the bird. On spotting it, I should have decelerated my car carefully to a full stop before reaching it, switched my emergency lights on, then picked it up and carried it safely to the shade under a tree on the grassed kerbside. May be it would have revived. All it would have taken me was less than a minute to do my rescue act.

As the traffic was very light at that time, the temporary closure of the lane would also not have caused much disruption to other road users, perhaps none at all. But I was not quick enough to deal with the sudden situation. I blame myself, and not the other driver, for causing the poor bird's crushing death on the road.

> *In the distant past, morality, ethics and justice used to be considered as virtues, but now these words figure only in text books and school lessons. In the present time, might, deceit and trickery are the order of the day. People learn these traits from home and powerful people. Politicians use these weapons*

unashamedly. If misleading, cooked and blatant lies, and half-truths, can get the job done, why not?

Thinking about it, how ironical is it that mass killers, who claim to fight for any mission, howsoever noble or just that mission may be, cause and contribute to immense, irreparable damage to the mission and the image of their own community they claim to represent. The killers selfishly ignore the fact that there will be serious repercussions from their violent acts, which their community members will have to face.

People Move on After Your Use-by Date

For nearly five decades, while her selfless, noble husband—a renowned teacher of Transcendental Meditation (TM)—attended to the minds of tens of thousands of people—she tended to their bellies tirelessly, like a caring and loving mother, when they visited their teacher. She was a kind, warm and loving person, a mother to the people who sought her husband's help. She had been a school teacher in her younger days.

Every day, she cooked and served lunches, dinners, tea and coffee (with snacks) to scores of people who visited her husband for learning TM, weekly Thursday prayers, regular discourses etc. Her supporting role to her husband had become significantly prominent after the exodus of Kashmiri Pandits from their home in 1990. Her husband selflessly tried to help tens of thousands of displaced Kashmiri Pandits—at Jammu and in Delhi—in regaining reasonable degree of sanity and reclaiming their lives. Understandably, after their exodus, they were suffering from deep grief and an irreversible shock of losing their ancestral home and hearth, some to a point of insanity.

When she died about six years after the death of her esteemed husband, her funeral was attended by just about 30 people, which included her immediate family members and the author. Obviously, the number of attendees was disproportionately far less than the number of people whom she and her husband had served in her life. That is life; people move on after your use-by date.

> *We are seen as sheer commodities till we are resourceful and influential, and of some use to other people, beyond which we are seen as liabilities by the same very people who may have benefited from us or been close to us to prosper. People move on after they realise you are past your use-by date.*
>
> *People will stick to you as long as you are a fruit-bearing tree or a cow that gives milk. Once you stop bearing fruit or giving milk, you will be felled or killed, as the case may be, and used for other things.*

Betrayal Under the Garb of Love

A 26-year old cab driver (Class 8th) married his sweetheart (BA, Part 2), from his native village in Bihar, at the age of 18, surprisingly without the permission and attendance of his parents or other members of his family at his wedding.

On being asked why he had done so, he said his wife was the only child of her parents, and added: *Hum kya aaloo chap hun, aise hee shaadi karte? Jab ghar aur biwi dono mile, tabhi to shaadi ki, chhod ke na hi chale jaate usko?* (*Am I a hillbilly? When I got a home and a wife too, I decided to marry; would I have not otherwise abandoned her?*) A smart go-getter, who used love for material benefits! He intended to reclaim his inheritance from his family.

In another case, a 50-year old cab driver, from Bihar, previously in a managerial position in a multi-national automobile company said:

I loved my younger brothers so much and looked after them. I would spend lots of money on them. I would not eat my dinner till they returned home from work in the evening and joined me. I was flying very high; I did not care for money or God. I had become too confident and arrogant. But God taught me a lesson and I crashed, not only to the ground but even sank below the ground surface. Now I am slowly reclaiming my life backs. I am determined to make much more progress than I had made earlier.

I have become humble and wise. I have also learnt how selfish people can be, and how callous and unpredictable this world can be.

My own two brothers, who are doing well in their lives, suddenly turned their back on me when I desperately needed their support; they thought I was going to be a liability for them.

Conscience and Corruption

Corruption kills conscience. One evening, at a bus stop, as he waited for the bus to go home, he felt very hungry and tired. He noticed a fancy restaurant across the road buzzing with people. He felt sad. He wished he had enough money in his purse to afford some food at that restaurant.

Just an hour ago, he had paid a hefty sum of money—as bribe, from his hard earned salary—to an officer at a government department, as 'incentive' for 'locating' his father's 'lost' pension file. As he struggled to cope with his fatigue, hunger and frustration, he noticed the same officer and his family gleefully stepping out of a cab and heading into that restaurant.

Self-Worship

While some can't stop praising themselves and taking credit for the work done by others, some can't stop praising others and giving credit to them. While some can't spare time from serving people, some have no time to serve anyone except themselves.

Real happiness lies in praising others and giving credit to deserving people. *Attention, adoration, admiration and affection are the 4 'A's that keep most of us going.* Not many of us are saints and detached from the world.

Keeping Appearances

People generally judge others based on their appearances and not necessarily on who they are. It takes a lifetime to know one but just a moment to see one.

On social media, you will get a 100 or more 'thumbs up' for posting your picture with professionally dyed hair and wearing a confident smile and a flashy designer suit, dining at an expensive restaurant. But not many will understand or appreciate your thought.

Appearances are deceptive and tend to fool others. Most people fall for what they see with their eyes. People generally worship others for what they show they have, and not for what they actually are.

Keeping appearances does not always work for very long. The moment you open your mouth in an assembly of intelligent and wise people, you will be judged for who you actually are; your jewellery, make-up or dress won't help to hide the real you.

How Can We Judge Others?

We sell what we have. We sell our soul and conscience, time, intellect, wisdom, experience, expertise, skills, art, physical strength, looks, charm, body shape and body. Some of us may be called prostitutes in a traditional sense, but what about the others? We take risks, both adventurous and calculated. Some of us are called gamblers, but what about others?

We manipulate the system and other people into maximising our benefits. Some of us, especially the poorer ones, are called beggars, but what about others? Aren't there wealthy beggars? We cheat and steal from the system, government and individuals. Some of us are called thieves, but what about the others? Isn't corruption a mix of prostitution, gambling, begging and stealing? Who are we then? Why do we judge others if we are all same to a lesser or greater extent?

Life Varies its Pace

As a child, I wished to quickly grow up. My joy knew no bounds when I turned ten. Similar was the case when I turned 20. I thought adults enjoyed absolute freedom. The day I turned 30, I lived one of the saddest days of my life. My 40th birthday anniversary came and went, without any emotional feelings. It was just another day in my busy life. By then, I had been working like a mule to support my young family overseas. I was greatly desensitised by then to those little thrills and frivolities of life. At 50, I took a new stance in my life, similar to what a batsman does on scoring a ton. It was time to take a fresh look at my life, as not much time was left for me. I started running every day and reduced my food by half, losing about 16 kg in 8 months. Some people (silently) thought, perhaps, I had lost weight due to cancer. At 52, I started writing and haven't looked back since. Robert Frost said: "The woods are lovely, dark and deep; but I have promises to keep and miles to go before I sleep."

Writing

When you write, write for humans. Write for good causes, write for future generations. Write to unify the world. Be true to yourself. Let your words ooze from your heart, from your soul. Be fearless, be pure. Do not fear being judged by others. Let the future judge you.

Written words survive the test of time, some last for generations, some for centuries and some for several millennia. Let your words speak the God's language—fair and just. Let your words be the drops of life-giving nectar, and not the drops of poison.

> *Your words have no merit if they are aimed to divide the world and cause strife. Your words are hollow if they are aimed to appease others to win you favours, power and wealth.*
>
> *Never write if you do not believe in your words. Never write if you do not have convictions in your thoughts. Never write if you do not have scruples against unfairness and injustice.*

We Belong to the World

In 1983, my Kashmiri taxi driver—after picking me up from the airport—spoke with me only in English. He thought I was an English tourist on holiday.

In 1985, a couple of West-Asian students in Kashmir spoke with me in their language but I responded in English. Their facial expressions changed into disbelief.

In 1987, most rickshaw pullers, shopkeepers and our milkman in Roorkee (UP, India) communicated with me in English. They all thought I was a foreigner.

In 1995, a chirpy Malay taxi driver in Kuala Lumpur thought I was a *matsale'* (English).

In 1997, a shopkeeper in Jammu (India) asked me in English where I was from, although I spoke with him in Hindi. He refused to accept I was from anywhere in India.

In 1998, a group of Middle-Eastern looking youth were frustrated and intrigued when I did not respond to them in their language.

In 2000, an early-morning lemon vendor in Jammu continued to communicate with me in good English though I kept speaking with him in Hindi.

Since 1997, many people in Australia take me for a South African. My Iranian colleagues believe I'll pass easily as an Iranian in their country.

My mother would tell me that my maternal grandfather would often say that my rights were secure and reserved around the world. I was meant to belong to the world.

Happiness

There are some tricky situations in life, where your loss is certain. For example, if your parents (or even children) are publicly contesting against each other, your loss is certain regardless of who wins.

If your world is all about yourself and your happiness is hedonic, you will only look for your wins. Thus, you will see it as a case of assured win, from one side or the other, regardless of who wins or loses. You are, therefore, a survivor. However, if your world is also about others (altruistic), you will also suffer for the loss of others. In case of altruistic happiness (i.e. about others), it will be seen as a case of assured loss regardless of which one of them wins. It will be hard for altruistic people to celebrate the win of one parent (or child) while the other parent (or child) is mourning the loss.

Most of us——exercising a basic survival instinct——cling to the rays of hope and the possibilities of individual wins. We keep chasing happiness——in all its shapes and forms—through the satisfaction of all our five senses. Humans have learnt how to survive and look after their individual self. However, it is also true that our very tendency to chase happiness also thwarts our happiness. We keep looking for it outside of us, through the satisfaction of our five senses, without looking for it inside us.

Attempt to suicide—anywhere in the civilised world—is a serious crime. It carries a jail term. We can't just talk about it so lightly and get away. To take your life or anyone else's life are both serious crimes. Suicide is blasphemous, a sin and an act of crime against one's parents, God, humanity and the millions of medical researchers and practitioners, both past and present, who strive day and night for saving lives. Suicide is akin to a soldier irresponsibly abandoning his / her border post.

If there were no poor people, no one would work for anyone. Will, therefore, the rich and the powerful support zero poverty? Capitalism flourishes on two laws of the animal kingdom: 'Might is right' and 'survival of the fittest'. Our house and clothes define us. Fancy designs represent complex-minded people. Simple designs represent depth and authenticity.

The word 'Hindu' is most likely alien for the people living in the land of Indus, India. Most probably, it did not exist in the first millennium. Anecdotally, the name 'Hindu' was first coined and used by the Arabs or Turks for the people of the subcontinent (Bharat). The historical Persian name for India is 'Hindustan'. In ancient Bharat, the religious philosophy was perhaps termed as Sanatan Dharam, or perhaps not. Perhaps there was no name for the religious philosophy. Gentlemen in northern Bharat would address one another as 'arya'.

Humans pretend to be the most sophisticated and intelligent species on the earth. Despite their tall claims about their cultural sophistication and civilisation, they are actually the most mean and dangerous animals on the planet. Not only do they consume and destroy all other life forms and the environment mindlessly, but they also devour their own kind, one way or the other. Humans are the most greedy, selfish, manipulating and conniving creatures on the planet. Interestingly, a small number of them unselfishly strive to be different, perhaps due to their greater degree of evolution than the rest.

Humans have never stopped being territorial. They will never stop fighting one another. Whenever and wherever they feel threatened or endangered—physically, financially, socially, ethnically, professionally, religiously or just for purely egotistical reasons—they react. They use all means available to them—power and authority, or arms and weapons, or electronic and social media these days—to overcome, destroy and annihilate their enemies, both real and perceived.

> *Till humans exist on the earth, they will never stop fighting. They will find reasons to fight one another. Anger, greed and violence are ingrained in them. The conniving animal inside them always gets the better of their sophisticated exterior. Their civility gives in to their violent core. Wars—both territorial and trade—will continue till humans exist.*
>
> *In tricky situations, it takes just one moment during which we make that life-changing choice which decides the course of our future life. It takes just one moment beyond which life never remains the same. After that one moment, we sink or swim.*

Deteriorating World Order

Many ask why the world has turned out the way it is at the present—polarised, jingoistic, selfish and materialistic, marked with much lesser personal, professional and political loyalties and a stark absence of world statesmen and benevolent leaders. They forget that the present world is the resultant of all past human actions—individual and combined. Our past has shaped our present world. But it will not stay this way, it will keep changing. As everything else, our world order will follow a more circular path and return to where we started from, as nothing in this world moves in a straight line.

Our world order will continue to deteriorate and crumble to attain its lowest possible point—in morality and ethics (civil, social, political, and environmental) before turning back upward. The current inter and intra social and national stresses—due to strategic and political interests for enjoying supreme domination over others—will dissipate but only after facing their logical consequences. Some of us will destroy it extensively before those who survive painstakingly rebuild it from scratch, slowly, bit by bit over the next few millennia. Phoenix will rise.

But for the possible destruction—as a logical design of Nature but exercised through us humans, who are also a part of Nature—our planet will not be able to sustain our continued growth, our menacingly growing footprint and the damage we have been causing to Nature to meet our unabated demands for our survival, albeit many more selfish ends. The human footprint must reduce and the human population must reduce to a more sustainable level, such as in the first millennium.

> *Anything that we do against Nature—unintentionally out of ignorance, or intentionally out of greed, or foolishness—is construed as a sin. No sin goes unpunished, no matter how much we pray to Nature. Nature is blind—in giving and in taking.*
>
> *We have to pay the price for our sins, quite a heavy price. Nature levels off everything before regenerating life. Reconstruction will follow destruction. Stability will follow instability but only after the damage is done.*

Social Hierarchy and Class System

Large passenger planes model the general world socio-economical order and power hierarchy. Although all passengers are exposed to a similar risk profile and travel to the same destination, their individual class in the plane—Business Class, First Class, Premium Economy Class, Economy Class—defines the level of treatment they receive on board. The more your pay for your ticket, the more attention you will receive, with equally better services. It does not matter who pays for your ticket—you, or the organisation you work for, or the tax-payer—or how you pay for your ticket—through honest money or the money earned through corruption—your money will talk. Money talks!

> *Wealth corrupts and tends to justify the end. It blinds us to social discrimination and exploitation, which is the greatest blasphemy against Nature. We forget the other person, who we think is inferior to us, —due to status, power or wealth, is similar to us in flesh and blood. It is reason for most social evils.*

Live in the Moment

O flower, when you were born, you were small, folded and protected, you were called a bud. You looked sleepy and you were left to sleep in your home; no one liked to pluck you away and use you for prayers or decorations. No wind could blow you away unless it snapped the branch on which you were born.

As you grew, you opened up and blossomed with happiness. People adored you. Your beauty became a cause of your separation from your home and abuse.

Some plucked you off and used you for their rituals and decorations for some time before you were disposed of in rubbish bins or immersed in water bodies. In some cases, however, when you were at the peak of your youth, strong winds suddenly blew away your beautiful petals, leaving you poor and naked till a gardener pruned you away, as no one liked you.

Where you were lucky, you aged slowly in your home—the branch on which you were born—till your petals wilted slowly and fell away one by one. All through your life, you had no control on your life. You were used, abused and crushed under feet by man or blown away by nature. Only a few of you were fortunate to have lived a full life.

Life is whimsical, coincidental and unpredictable. It teaches us time and again why we must try to live in the moment and never take the next moment or hour for granted.

Life may be short or long, but it is never easy or perfect. Struggles and challenges define it, pain and suffering characterise it. A life that is lived by facing its challenges, and fearlessly fighting to overcome them, is a life lived full, a life lived well, irrespective of its failures and successes, and whether it is short or long.

Are life and the world real or illusion? No one really knows! Surely, however, everything is transitory. It is only up us to make some sense of it while it is fast passing us. Sense or no sense, it is what it is.

A Moment in Life

In that one moment, when an earthquake struck, he decided to leave the building just before it collapsed. He saved his life.

In that one moment, when the clouds thundered and it started pouring heavily, he decided to apply brakes. He saved a child from being run over. He saved a life.

In that one moment, he decided to accelerate his car when he saw another car speeding fast towards him. He avoided a serious collision and saved lives. He also saved his life.

In that one moment, when he felt uneasy and uncertain about the deal, he decided to walk out of an important business meeting. He saved his home and fortune. He saved his life.

In that one moment, he decided to cancel his holiday and jumped out of his train just as it started to move. He saved his job and his career. He saved his life.

In that one moment, he decided to apologise to his wife after their overheated argument turned extremely ugly. He saved his marriage. He saved his life.

In that one moment, he decided not to take the flight when the radio announced a severe weather warning. His plane crashed. He saved his life.

In that one moment, he decided to forgo his dinner and observe a fast. He saved himself from food poisoning and missing the flight of his life. He lived on.

In that one moment, he decided not to sign the contract to buy that expensive house. He saved himself from becoming bankrupt. He lived on.

In that one moment, he lost total self-control, took out his gun and killed the other person. He became a murderer and spent the rest of his life in jail. His lost his life.

In that one moment, he lost his mental balance and decided to break his marriage. He lost his home and a loving wife. He lost his life.

Keep the doors and windows of your mind open

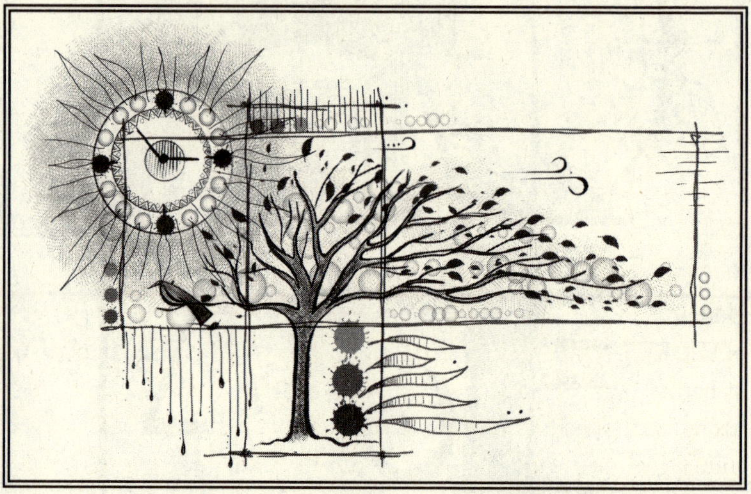

Bide your time when the wind of time blows against you

TWO

THE PHILOSOPHY OF LIFE

Nature Respects Strength and Power

NATURE DOES NOT respect the weak and the meek. As per law of nature, weaker life-forms are consumed (mercilessly) by relatively strong and powerful ones. Plants hardly put up any defence against animals, although some plants are known to be carnivores. Animals consume plants—fruits, vegetables, roots, herbs etc. In the rest of the animal kingdom, animals follow the food chain. If lions do not hunt and devour their prey, they will not be able to survive; they too are finally consumed by other animals when they grow old and weak. In some situations, even their slightest hesitation, or self-doubt, during their attack on their prey can potentially cost them their lives. This natural law remains valid and applicable for humans too.

To be gentle or humble does not necessarily mean being virtuous. Virtuosity requires gentleness interwoven with strength and bravery and, most importantly, the willingness to use one's strength and power for selfless noble causes, including winning justice for others and helping the downtrodden and defenceless. Strength is the greatest deterrence against being exploited or consumed by others. In the animal kingdom, many animals have evolved over time and learnt ways to protect themselves through various survival skills, such as camouflage, creating frightening sounds, spewing venom, vibratory body movements, spiking, fanning etc.

Passive aggression may be considered as the best form of defence to ward off nasty aggressors. Nuclear capability may currently be saving many nations who, otherwise, would have been punished (by more powerful nuclear nations) for their misdeeds or for not towing their line. In hindsight, if Iraq had nuclear capability, its history over the past couple of decades would have been entirely different. Some other nations, who may have learnt from the Iraq episode, are believed or known to have silently developed their own nuclear capabilities—to a lesser or greater extent—with the aim to avoid meeting the same fate as Iraq.

Majority rules, it always has. It is always one, or a few, against many. And, invariably, many prevail. The onus is always on that one, or those few, to toe the line of the many and assimilate with them. Social media has clearly proven the herd mentality and animal behaviour of humans. In reality, it does not matter if you think you are right; what matters is if those many agree with you or not. Once the majority feels challenged and threatened by you, they will pounce on you as a group and try to tear you apart, just as those big cats—lions, tigers, cheetahs, leopards and hyenas—attack and kill much larger animals (elephants, rhinos, hippos and buffaloes) who get separated from their herd.

Might is right. Bigger fishes eat smaller fishes. Similarly, bigger business entities take over smaller businesses. In the real world, it is always a battle for dominance. Armies, institutions and organisations follow command and hierarchy. Even families are run as dictatorships till adolescents rebel and leave. Boss is always right. Social and professional hierarchies are also based on the principles of authority and power. Bravery and strength are respected. Cowardice is mocked at and looked down upon in most situations. All animals, including humans, bow to power. Lions and jackals don't command the same respect in the animal kingdom. Humans also regard them differently. Scavengers are generally shy and much weaker as individuals; they feed on the kill of others.

Gentler and weaker people (and communities) are generally exploited and abused by relatively more powerful individuals (and communities) as sheer commodities. Weak and poor people generally work for the strong and wealthy. In the present world of aggressive materialistic competition, meekness is generally construed as cowardice. To be powerful and strong—morally, educationally, financially, politically and physically—and yet be gentle and humble is being virtuous and noble. If so-called gentle people don't stand against injustice, oppression or terror, but instead lie low and hide, they can be considered as cowards. If so-called gentle people cannot protect themselves and their kin, can they be anyone's true friends? They may even compromise the wellbeing and safety of others and, therefore, can never be trusted.

Powerful people tend to test the power of others to mark their territory, similar to the behaviour of other animals. They have two options of when and how to use their strength; of those, one leads to glory and the other to disaster. Those powerful people who choose not to display their strength and power in vain or to frighten others or misuse it for their selfish ends are acknowledged and glorified in history as real heroes. But those who misuse their strength and power to deliberately oppress and exploit others—as a result of their misguided beliefs or sadistic mental orientation or even a naturally evil disposition—go down in history as tyrants. History condemns them during their lifetime and long after they are gone. Cowards and bullies sadistically harass gentler people.

Nature is most powerful and, from time to time, it keeps reminding us about its infinite strength. Nature is also bountiful; it provides and nurtures all life species, without bias. Air and water are fine examples of strength and virtuosity. Life is not possible without both. Both are invisible in their natural states. As they look harmless and least threatening when they don't move, ignorant fools consider them as weak. But the wise have realised and know their strength. When air and water move with purpose, nothing can stand against them; they can uproot everything in their path. A bucketful of water is sufficient for drowning a giant. Let us, therefore, learn from nature and be strong to protect ourselves, yet be empathetic, caring and compassionate for other less-fortunate and weaker cohabitants.

A story titled, *Wolf and Lamb*, ends with a moral, 'might is right.' This story and its moral are valid and applicable to the current human jungle world too. People who are capable of thinking are usually snubbed, criticised and punished by other, relatively less capable people who generally comprise the bulk in any community. Socrates is one such excellent example of such thinkers. Many people foolishly believe ignorance is bliss and, in believing so, they undermine themselves. Such people also tend to worship material wealth, and the wealthy and powerful people. A country where such people are in a majority never prospers or progresses. It is because of them that democracy is misused by a very small percentage of clever and conniving individuals who also end up ruling them.

> *Humans are whimsical and temperamental. Their emotions, likes and dislikes are never constant and keep changing as the moon waxes and wanes, as tides rise and fall, as seasons change, as day moves into night and back into day. Their thoughts even differ before and after eating meals, as well as before and after undertaking a journey.*
>
> *Our present is shaped by our current and past actions, inactions and experiences. Our body changes constantly too. Today, I am not essentially the same person as I was yesterday. Tomorrow too, I'll not be the same person as I am today.*

Your Power Will Destroy You if You Are Not Wise

It is said '*absolute power corrupts absolutely*'. In your corrupted form, you will become arrogant, overconfident, boisterously proud and ruthless. You will develop a short fuse and tend to lose your temper on facing even the smallest challenges and provocations from your critics. You will tend to speak without thinking, as your thinking capability will be eroded. You will be drunk and intoxicated with power. You will become mentally imbalanced and stagger just like a heavily drunk alcoholic.

Once you are corrupted absolutely, your doom is certain and it is only a matter of time before that happens. In the scheme of things, you, as an individual, don't really matter, except to yourself and your family, and your doom will be of no consequence to anyone, again, except to yourself and your family. But, as it happens more often than not, before you really bite the dust and disappear, you will have caused immense damage to many other people because you don't exist in isolation. You are a part of several systems—family, community, organisation, country and the wider world.

The extent of damage that you will possibly cause depends on how tall you are in terms of your stature (professional, social and political) and, therefore, how wide is your circle of influence. The higher you are, the greater will be the extent of the damage that you will potentially cause to others. History is full of examples of many such corrupted powerful individuals who caused immense damage to the world during their lifetime and long after their death.

Power on its own is highly whimsical, unstable, inflammable and volatile. It uses you without taking any blame on itself. It will make you do many wrong things when you are intoxicated. An unholy combination of unbridled power and immense wealth is the most dangerous cocktail and a toxic recipe for disaster. It will cost you your head, destroy your judgement and prudence, and bring you, and the wider world, nothing but doom.

With power, therefore, it will be extremely imprudent to mix wealth. Prudence demands that wealth be kept away from power, just as a lighter is kept away from petrol or matches are kept away from gunpowder. Instead, mix power with wisdom so that it can be kept under heavy check and used solely for noble, selfless causes.

Learn how nuclear power is kept carefully under check for reasons of unacceptable consequences.

Therefore, if you have the blessings of Goddess Durga, the Hindu goddess of power, and are drenched in power and strength, it will be prudent for you to also worship Goddess Saraswati, the goddess of knowledge, instead of following Goddess Laxmi, the goddess of wealth. Past generations of Pandits in Kashmir firmly believed and advised their children: '*If you follow Saraswati, Laxmi will follow you. But if you follow Laxmi, Saraswati will abandon you.*'

In a nutshell, Kashmiri Pandits advocated that wisdom and knowledge could always bring you wealth and prosperity but wealth alone would not make you wise, and because wisdom is essential for your overall progress, follow Saraswati. Note that *Intelligence* and *wisdom* are two entirely different terms. Intelligence can work in both positive and negative domains but wisdom only operates within a positive domain. There can be intelligent criminals, villains and demons, but there can only be wise saints.

In conclusion, your preference between Saraswati and Laxmi will decide whether you will become a saint or a demon, a hero or a villain, a leader or a tyrant. Figuratively, Saraswati will help you as a probiotic when you take antibiotics, or like a coolant in a radiator that keeps a hot engine cool and healthy. Choose wisely and write your destiny. Ethics tells us 'moral is right'. But as per politics, 'might is right.' When politics wins, humanity loses. What an irony! Wise and intelligent people waste their precious time in discussing hopeless issues and powerful people! An extreme gives birth to another extreme. For stability, it is best that one stays in the middle.

If there were no poor people, no one would work for anyone. Will the upper twenty-percent richer people ever support zero poverty? Capitalism flourishes on two laws of the animal kingdom: 'might is right' and 'survival of the fittest.

Guns harm everyone, always. They puts dust on the core issues. No one has ever benefited from the gun, except the gun sellers. What a sincere dialogue can achieve, a gun can never achieve. Peaceful and persistent negotiations are the way to resolve issues. Guns have undoubtedly undermined the wellbeing of all Kashmiris, as statistics prove, but that is past. Let all well-meaning Kashmiris now come together and see what can be achieved. Reason and rationale have always worked, and always will.

Lord Krishna knew the outcome of the Mahabharata, so He did not give up negotiations until the last moment. Unashamedly, He went back and forth between the two parties to avoid war. Kauravas, who opted for His army (instead of Him), even tried to kill Him, so He had to reveal His true Cosmic identity. He knew that nothing would be left after the war and that is exactly what happened. Although Kauravas were defeated and killed, Pandavas did not win either although they survived. There was nothing left that they could rule over.

We spew what exists and is produced within us. Some are able to digest and process their raw thoughts—thanks to their growth, education, culture and sophistication, and accordingly shape their actions but most just throw it out raw, almost instinctively, like other life forms.

> *Life is a great leveller. Despite such a wide power differential across social hierarchy, it is only humbling, logical and just—and perhaps comforting for the most—that the privileged, powerful and famous people in the world also breed, eat, walk, talk, cry and die just as their vastly underprivileged, much weaker and little known counterparts.*
>
> *No human is more privileged and as resourceful or powerful than life and nature. Humans must realise this reality before they bite the dust.*

Humans Fight as They Live in Several Worlds

Physically, we may seem to be living in one world that we see with our eyes, hear with our ears and feel with our hands. Realistically, however, we live in several worlds, sometimes concurrently. Based on our individual beliefs and superstitions, perspectives and imaginations, knowledge and understanding of the cosmos, as well as our past memories and life experiences, our individual worlds practically differ. It is this difference between our individual worlds that causes strife between humans.

In the physical world that we see, scientific and natural laws prevail. However, in our unique, imaginary, non-visible worlds, we set our own (human) laws, which are shaped by our individual or collective beliefs, values, superstitions and fears. The laws that we create for ourselves work both ways—for and against us. Our beliefs, superstitions and fears affect our psychological world and we suffer internally, possibly due to guilt and remorse, when we break our self-created laws and, coincidently, bad things happen to us. In addition, when we try to impose our laws on others, peace becomes a casualty.

Physical world

In our physical world, based on the ongoing expansion of knowledge—through nonstop human endeavour to know the unknown and explore the untouched within the cosmic existence, using the tools as provided by the global education and research infrastructure related to all aspects of human life—humans should not logically be fighting one another over the veracity of the established natural and physical laws. However, some people still find reasons to fight one another based on the extent—depth and width—of their scientific knowledge, laws of nature and life experience.

Only a few centuries ago, many thinkers and scientific philosophers were challenged and harassed by the establishment of the time for putting forth their thoughts about the nature of the universe and its laws. Their thoughts challenged the way other humans thought (ignorantly) about the universe till then.

Nicolaus Copernicus (1473-1543), a Renaissance-era polyglot and polymath (mathematician, astronomer, physician, classics scholar, translator, governor, diplomat, and economist) formulated (just before his death) a revolutionary model of the universe, which put the Sun at the centre of the universe, with the Earth revolving around it. Until then, people were made to believe (by the establishment) that the Earth was at the centre of the universe and the Sun revolved around it. Copernicus was born and died in Royal Prussia, a region that had been a part of the Kingdom of Poland.

Giordano Bruno (1548-1600) an Italian Dominican friar (born Filippo Bruno), extended the work of Copernicus. He was a philosopher, mathematician, poet, cosmological theorist, and Hermetic occultist and known for his cosmological theories. He proposed that the stars were distant suns surrounded by their own planets. As cosmic pluralism, he also raised the possibility that these planets could foster life of their own. He insisted that the universe is infinite, without any centre. For his revolutionary thoughts (and heresy) that challenged the Catholic Church, he was tried for seven years (1593-1600) by the Roman Inquisition. He was charged with blasphemy and denial of several core Catholic doctrines, such as eternal damnation, the Trinity, the divinity of Christ, the virginity of Mary, and transubstantiation. The Church held grave concerns about his pantheism, as well as his teaching of the transmigration of the soul. On (Ash) Wednesday, 17 February 1600, he was hung upside down naked and then burnt. His ashes were thrown into the Tiber River.

At present, the flat Earth theory continues to be kept alive by some people whose beliefs continue to remain rooted in the medieval times. Many ancient cultures subscribed to a flat Earth cosmography till Aristotle provided evidence for the spherical shape of the Earth by around 330 BC. Despite the scientific facts available about the Earth's sphericity, pseudo-scientific flat Earth conspiracy theories continue to be driven by modern flat Earth societies and individuals using social media.

At present, many people don't believe that man really landed on the moon half a century ago.

Individual Worlds

Our private worlds are born the moment we are born and start recording memories. Our internal world disappears suddenly when we stop breathing. It is just a bubble. Our internal world is uniquely our own. It is bound to clash with the internal world of other people because our internal worlds are also interwoven with beliefs and values from our other worlds—families, communities and nations.

When we close our eyes, we drift into a world which is uniquely our own private world. In this world, we are absolutely free to do anything we like. It is shaped by our memories and imaginations. In this world, we feel more secure and relatively more comfortable, because of our past memories. We can go anywhere we like to go, eat anything we want to and feel anything we want to feel all based on the memories of our past. We can punch anyone we hate and love anyone we love. It only requires us to close our eyes and drift in our private world where our laws prevail.

Each one of us 7.5 billion people on this planet lives in a unique internal world of our own, which is shaped by our imagination, perceptions, beliefs and superstitions. This world manifests as our personal nature and is faintly reflected by our personal tastes, likes and dislikes; personal interests, passions and hobbies; and general orientations. We make our own laws for ourselves, based on our experiences and the repetition of experiences, imaginary causes and effects and, above all, fear.

Famous cricketers, of both the past and present, are known to have a superstitious routine, eg putting a red handkerchief in their right pocket, wearing left pad first, putting the left foot forward while crossing the boundary line to bat, frequent (nervous) withdrawal of hands from batting gloves, frequent rotation of bat etc. Elements of superstitions are also seen in other sportspersons, as well as the rich and famous. People avoid wearing certain colours on certain days of the week and occasions, and show preference for particular colours that have proved to be lucky in the past.

Family Worlds

Families usually have their own unwritten laws and superstitions, which they term as family values. For example, some families demand their children have matrimonial alliances within their own ethnic communities or within their own socio-economic classes. Interestingly, the author's family does not make sundried pickles because of some bad experiences of earlier generations. Due to fear of (imaginary) repercussions, subsequent generations have followed the unwritten law and never dared to make pickles.

Community Worlds

A community can comprise people belonging to the same religion, ethnicity, caste, gender, calling, sport and socio-economic class. Humans have tendency to get polarised within communities, which generally ends in dividing them between 'us' and 'them', invariably with mutual apprehensions, driven mainly by threat and fear.

Every community follows certain ways of doing things, based on its beliefs and values. In the cricketing world, number 13 is considered as unlucky. As such, batsmen try to jump this number for fear of getting out on this number. Chinese community considers number '4' as a bad number (signifying death) and number '8' as a good number (signifying prosperity). As such, floor levels 4, 14 and 24 in any multi-storey building in SE Asia, and perhaps in the mainland China, are denoted usually as floor levels 3A, 13A and 23A respectively. Kashmiri Pandits don't traditionally consume mutton, fish or eggs on the 8th day of the waxing moon (Ashtami); however, they do consume mutton and fish on Navreh (The Kashmiri Pandit New Year day) and Haerath (Shivratri). Reverse is the case with other Hindus of India.

Interestingly, people from one community generally tend to criticise people from other communities, and sometimes scoff at them for following and nurturing outdated beliefs and values without realising they too follow similar outdated beliefs and values themselves.

Nationalism

Nationalism separates a nation from other nations when it claims to be the greatest of all. But who measures it and what are the parameters based on which it can be measured and claimed to be great? Do military might and wealth of a country make a nation great? If yes, humans have not progressed since the dark ages. Real human progress would be deemed to have occurred when no one nation claims superiority over other nations, but instead treats all other nations with equal dignity and respect.

Through history, humans have been reaping the fruits of hard work undertaken by people from many other countries across the world, and not only from their own country. Let us just look at the engineered world around us, including the appliances and gadgets that we use constantly, which have been developed and, perhaps manufactured, in other countries.

Nations import humans from other countries, be it as manual labourers, or as technicians, or scientists, or as other professionals. Nations also import food, medicines and technology from other nations. When a nation launches a satellite in space, or announces any other significant scientific breakthrough, how often does its leadership acknowledge and thank the conceptual inputs and the foundation works undertaken by the pioneers of the space technology, and the hard work of scientists and engineers from those pioneering countries who made such space missions possible? The answer is: 'Not very often, mainly due to nationalism and national pride. We don't like to give credit to others. We tend to use others but choose to live in our own bubble of nationalism.'

Nationalism is, however, different from national characteristics, the latter defining the general thinking and behaviours of people. Traditions mark the uniqueness of a country. For example, New Zealanders exhibit their unique character by the *haka*, a Mauri ceremonial dance (or rather a challenge), which is performed by a group, with vigorous movements and stamping of the feet, with rhythmically shouted accompaniment. Historically associated with traditional battle preparations of male warriors, the *haka* is performed by both men and women at social functions, including sporting events, welcoming distinguished guests, or to acknowledge great achievements, or at funerals.

To conclude, therefore, it is not surprising that humans fight one another when their worlds clash. Their fights are based on their religious beliefs, fears and apprehensions (valid or unfounded), superstitions, value systems and nationalism. Such fights will continue till the human race exists on the planet. Recognition of this reality is important so as to bring some acceptable degree of mutual tolerance and respect amongst humans, which is essential for their peaceful coherence on this unique planet.

There can never be one world for humans because they are not robots. Their internal worlds are as infinite as the outer world they live in. Every human is a complete cosmos in himself or herself.

When your thoughts on matters of social and national importance differ consistently and contrastingly from the thoughts of most other people, either you are blinded to reality or something extremely terrible is imminent. It is true winner takes it all. It is also true that the manner in which one wins or loses defines one's character. Fairness and justice in victory, or defeat, and treating one's opponent with respect and dignity are the hallmarks of a true champion.

Those people who compulsively think mainly about themselves, putting themselves at the centre of the world, or are generally selfish by their nature remain unhappy for most of the time in their life. From time to time, they believe the whole world is about them, after them, for them and against them. In short, for them, it is only me, me, me! So long as their focus does not move to some purpose in life, preferably selfless and noble, away from themselves, they never enjoy pure happiness.

How surprising it is that I have met and tried to be a friend to hundreds of people in my life but the actual number of people who have been my friends has remained equal to the number of fingers of my hand. I am still my own best friend (and worst enemy).

How fortunate I have been to be able to stand, walk and run on my legs; to be able to bathe, brush my teeth, eat and shave using my hands; and, most importantly, to be able to read and write. Nature has been very kind to me in this lifetime. This sheer realisation is truly humbling.

I must remain grateful for the gifts that I have received in this lifetime or the Giver will laugh at me. How can I take anything for granted?

Humans must eat to survive. Human mouth smells, at least after waking up in the morning. Human excreta smell. We stink if we don't bathe every day. How can some of us consider ourselves as superior to the other human beings? Everyone goes back to dust.

> *The human thought differentiates one human from the other. Some think deeply, most can't. Some give, most take. Some work for others, most work for themselves. Only some are happy, most crave for it. Happiness comes when one works for others, selflessly. That happiness is deep and long lasting.*
>
> *Humans are born from humans and without the human effort, no humans have or can ever be born. All humans have the same anatomy and breed the same way regardless of where or to whom they are born.*

To Err is Human, to Forgive Divine

"To err is human, to forgive divine," goes an old English saying, from a poem, *An Essay on Criticism*, by Alexander Pope (1688–1744), a famous English writer. Two more famous quotes are also from his poems: (a) *A little learning is a dangerous thing;* and (b) *Fools rush in where angels fear to tread.*

The first of the above three quotes could be useful in freeing oneself from the *karmic* cycle and, thereby, save oneself from a perpetual cycle of constant suffering, caused due to a natural human tendency to react, via a *tit for tat* policy. Reactionary acts of giving and taking—*punishment*, *grief*, *pain* and *revenge*—plunge one into an eternal cycle of suffering. The one and the only way to come out of the cycle is to forgive. Otherwise, if one believes in taking revenge or punishing the other person, one must also be prepared to receive a reaction in the future, possibly harsher. A policy of revenge brings nothing but eternal doom; it never ends and the cycle continues.

Those people, who believe in the Hindu philosophy of reincarnation, must accept that anything that happens to them now, or would have happened to them in the past, could have happened as a result of their own *karma*, either during this life or their past lives, which they don't remember. Forgiveness is the best medicine to rid oneself of the effects of the *karmic* cycle. There is no other better way than that.

One of the most important messages from the Bhagwad Gita is: *Surrender the fruit of your action to Me (Lord Krishna)*. This advice also helps one to attain freedom from the *karmic* cycle and the expectations arising from one's good deed. A wise old saying goes: *Do good and forget*. In north India, this saying goes like this: *Kar bhala aur dariya mein daal* (*Do good and offer it to the river*). Expectations are a recipe to discord and suffering.

In the Mahabharata, Lord Krishna did not fight for either of the two parties; He was solely on the side of *dharma* (righteousness, justice). As for His love, there is no evidence that he loved Duryodhana less than Arjuna. He offered Duryodhana the first pick but, unwisely, Duryodhana chose Lord Krishna's army instead of Him. Lord Krishna's army, therefore, fought on the side of the Kauravas. He became the charioteer of Arjuna, and that is how the Bhagwad Gita took birth. At the end of the war, no one effectively won, as nothing was left to be ruled after such mass destruction on all sides. Violence brings nothing but destruction.

The Pandavas lost their kingdom and were exiled only because they unwisely gambled away everything. They paid a heavy price for their own *karma*. The wise Pandava king, Yudhishthira, was aware they were being tricked by Shakuni, the Gandhar king during the gambling session. Lord Krishna also knew everything but the gambling session continued. At no stage, did He intervene and stop the session. His only intervention came at the time of Draupadi's *vastraharan*. As a wise king, Yudhishthira ought to have known that one, especially a king, must not gamble away one's kingdom, brothers, wife and himself. A king carries no such freedom or luxuries.

In the Ramayana, Lord Ram freed his consort, Sita, after His victory over mighty King Ravana. Whilst carrying Himself with such dignity and grace, Lord Ram never insulted King Ravana. He knew Ravana's calibre and had respect for his knowledge. Lord Ram gave all due respect to King Ravana even after the latter's defeat in the war, despite the latter's crime. Before embarking on their return journey to Ayodhaya, as the 14-year period of His exile had come to an end, two things happened:

- Sita was asked to take the *agni-pariksha* (fire-test) to prove her purity, which could be disputed and argued even now; and
- Lord Ram requested His father, King Dashrath (who had appeared from His heavenly abode to bless Him on his victory) to forgive his (step) mother, Queen Kaikeyi. Why? Because, He and Queen Kaikeyi knew the truth. She is believed to have been the main brain behind the plot to get rid of King Ravana from the earth, for his colossal arrogance and trespasses.

Queen Kaikeyi loved Lord Ram. And she was not alone; everyone loved Lord Ram for His virtues. He exemplified the prefect man—the *Purushottam*. Those who love him intertwine their every breath with his beautiful name. Every cell of theirs carries His name. Such people don't try to prove anything to anyone. Their noble deeds, without arrogance, reflect Lord Ram's grace and dignity.

On his Crucifixion, Lord Jesus Chris asked for forgiveness for his executioners. 'When they came to the place called The Skull, they crucified Him there, along with the criminals, one on His right and the other on His left. Then Jesus said, *"Father, forgive them, for they do not know what they are doing."* And they divided up His garments by casting lots. The people stood watching, and the rulers sneered at Him, saying, "He saved others; let Him save Himself if He is the Christ of God, the Chosen One."' … Luke 23:34

Forgiveness sets some humans apart from others. None of us is perfect; we make numerous trespasses in the course of a day. Empathy and care define human love. The following wise sayings are timeless and immortal:

- Do unto others as you would have them do unto you.
- Those who dig a pit for others themselves fall into it.
- What goes around comes around.
- As you sow, so shall you reap.
- Treat others as you wish to be treated by them.

The author's late mother, Jai Kishore Koul, instilled in him a number of virtues. Amongst her teachings are the following:

- Never wish bad for anyone, not even your worst enemies, as it may come back and haunt you one day. You never know the whole story—the bigger picture. You don't know what wrongs you may have done in your past lives.
- If you can't do good to anyone, don't try to do any bad also.
- If your right hand is helping anyone, your left hand must not know about it.

To conclude, the one and only mantra for breaking free from the karmic cycle and bringing peace is: Forgive (anyone who has troubled you) and forget (your personal good deeds).

Instant Karma

A well-educated, wise lady advised a concerned individual, "*Khao, piyo, mauj karo* (eat, drink and make merry), why waste time on such useless socio-political issues, people will do what they do!" How nice it would have been to live a cave life if our distant global ancestors had also followed a similar approach to life and living. Yesterday, she stopped her well-built son from helping their neighbour's daughter when she was openly being molested by a gang of ruffians. Today, she desperately cried for help when her own daughter was being molested by the same gang, but no one came to her help.

Our internal organisation is reflected by our external behaviour. A chaotic mind manifests in chaotic behaviour. For sustainable internal peace and a healthy organisation of our thoughts, therefore, it is important that we predominantly live in an environment of peace and organised habitat, or else the external chaos will inevitably make our inner world chaotic.

> *Internal peace is a fundamental requirement for enjoying both mental and physical health. It is also a core condition for attaining physical, spiritual and intellectual progress. When our internal environment synchronises with our external environment, our mind attains a state of stable equilibrium. A stable mind produces stable results.*
>
> *You think you will cleverly trick me and stealthily steal from me and I wouldn't know or do anything about it. You are wrong. You can't keep what does not belong to you. What you steal you will lose several times over, with penalty, to someone else. The process will continue till it returns to me, with interest, many times over. That is a natural law.*

Forgiveness—Various Perspectives

"The mistakes made by us inadvertently may not possibly stain our innocence. To err is human, so we may deserve forgiveness. But when we knowingly commit blunders that bring misery to many people, what do we call ourselves? Do we still deserve forgiveness?"

The author wrote the above and published it on social media. A fellow seeker, Mr Vijay Shankar—author, philosopher, journalist—while referring to Saul Bellow, an American-Canadian writer (1915-2005), winner of Nobel Prize, Pulitzer Prize and the National Medal of Arts—wisely responded:

"It is impossible to forgive if you don't believe in God … one must have faith that nature works out revenge. I remember this from Saul Bellow, an old favourite of mine in the eighties, and I think it is true. I mean we say God will punish or karma will punish …

There are two takes on this: One is that we get out of the way and, with a heightened sense of nobility and belief, we say 'we forgive'. But the second take is that, in reality, we don't want to forgive, instead we expect God or karma to punish the person. I feel, in truth, there is nothing like real forgiveness, the thing lingers. Only in extreme cases of one's belief in God, real forgiveness may be possible.

The case of Australian missionary, Graham Staines (1941-1999), comes to mind. He and his two pre-teen sons were sleeping in a van parked outside in the garden, as it was too hot inside the house, without electricity. A gang of religious extremists killed all three of them that night. They chained the doors of the van and set it on fire. Afterwards, his wife, Mrs Gladys Staines, left India. But, before she left, she said she had forgiven the murder accused, Dara Singh, who had led the attackers. I have never understood how she could forgive them, perhaps my failing."

Author: "You are very right. True forgiveness is associated with absolute faith in God. My take on Mrs Staines' forgiveness is:

When people truly forgive, they may really mean what they say about forgiving and forgiveness. Not only do they tend to purge themselves of toxicity from their mind, they also tend to hand over the case of delivering the justice to the higher Being—God, Nature—consciously or otherwise. And, perhaps, they may believe the higher justice is true, as only the higher Being knows the truth.

Dedicated missionaries, like Staines, work to uplift the underprivileged out of their miserable lives. Such people may have no socio-politico-religious motives, other than to dedicate their lives to the service of God's people. You may know the modern educational infrastructure in Kashmir was brought and established by missionaries. I have heard stories about nuns going from door to door in Srinagar and begging people to send their daughters to schools. But for them, one can imagine what would have been the state of educational infrastructure in Kashmir.

In 1947, nuns at St Joseph school, Baramulla, were amongst the earliest victims of rape and gruesome murder at the hands of tribal invaders from across the border. Srinagar's oldest schools—Tyndale-Biscoe School (since 1880), Mallinson Girls' School (since 1912), Presentation Convent Higher Secondary School (since 1936) and Burn Hall School (since 1942) were all founded and run by Christian missionaries."

Vijay Shankar: "Missionaries started the modern school system not only in Kashmir but also all over India. I respect the missionaries as even I got schooling at St Andrew's school in Bombay and then at St Stephens college in Delhi. I understand what you are saying. I wrote on the topic of forgiveness from the point of view of my personal observations and experience. To be truthful, I would not forgive if I was in Mrs Staines' shoes. I do not believe in God's justice or an ethical universe where everything happens for the best. I think the creative Principle (which is not a Man in the sksy) is an energy and natural intelligence, whom you might call the Being. But once created, man is literally on his own. He may do evil or good, and men have to cope with it. If you say God is fully responsible for everything, then He is also responsible for all the misery and cruelty in the world. I say no to that theory. I believe man is responsible for what he does and must cope with it. Sartre (Jean-Paul Sartre, a French philosopher, 1905-1980) said: *'Man is condemned to be free.'*

When we say God will punish an evil-doer, we outsource our revenge to God. That is all; the sense of revenge still remains there. This is an endless question. It is my reading of the Gita that evil must be fought and destroyed. Gandhi read non-violence into the Gita, which I do not agree with. Non-violence is a limited theory; it does not work in many cases. Anyway, I am just shooting the breeze!"

Author: "These are eternal questions. As Sartre said, *man is condemned to be free*, so these questions will always remain. I agree with you about the theory of the Being. But I believe the greatest revenge and the sole pathway to self-healing is indeed forgiveness. Yes, we tend to outsource our revenge to God, to free ourselves. I am in full agreement with your God concept. But I still have an element of belief in the theory of karma, but not sure for how long!"

Vijay Shankar: "We each have to work it out, I guess. Everything in spiritual matters is a belief. We know nothing."

Author: "Yes, we know nothing. And that truth has not changed since the days of Socrates. He always maintained that he knew nothing." With that, the chat concluded, at least till next time ...

Nothing is Everything, History Repeats Itself

What goes around comes around; that is karma. What goes up must come down; that is gravity. A day is followed by night and winter is followed by summer. Things keep going round and round.

We come from nothing and return to nothing, and that is the truth of life. That 'nothing' is 'everything', must be known as perhaps the greatest truth and purpose of human life. Otherwise, all other animals also eat and breed as we do. That 'nothing' drives the whole universe; it contains all secrets of life and existence. Figuratively, the way we must step into a shower without wearing clothes, when our number is called, we are left with no other choice but to walk alone into that 'nothing' without carrying our wealth and assets, family and friends, pride and position, or that stupid, stubborn, fat layer of ego that keeps us inflated lifelong into believing that we are 'something'. The fatter that layer of ego, the more disillusioned we are and farther we remain from the truth, and the more painful it will be to remove and throw it away when we must step into that 'nothing'.

None of the movements of our planets and moons are in a straight line. They keep returning to the point they start. Our life journey also replicates their movements. Our past reflects our future because one day we must return to it. World has never moved in a straight line, as civilisations have come and gone; they all shone in their days of glory at the zenith. Our present civilisation will also fall undoubtedly, thanks to the colossal arsenal of nuclear, chemical and biological weapons that we have amassed collectively around the globe for our own self-destruction. When and how, no one knows. It can happen any day as many powerful people around the world believe they are 'something'. It has happened before; humans are very intelligent but also extremely destructive. They connive and plan destruction. They destroy everything they create. But that may also be a law of Nature! Nature lives through its creation. Humans are a creation of Nature. No other life-form on earth is as dangerous and destructive as humans.

What is created must be destroyed. Figuratively, that is similar to how we thrive. All that we do in life is eventually flushed into those sewers or lands on dumping grounds. Most of us get education only to find jobs—to earn money—to buy facilities, home, clothes and food, all of which become unusable after some time and are disposed off. The best of food that we eat, after only a few hours, goes into a little pot in the toilet and is quickly flushed into the sewer.

All stars in the Milky Way live alone. Our sun and all planets in our solar system live alone. Our earth moves alone around the sun, so does our moon around our sun. They keep doing what they are destined to do, day and night, as we sleep. They may appear to be alone and independent but they are not independent; they are part of the solar system and, therefore, they must follow the laws of the system. Even their slightest disobedience or carelessness will be catastrophic for them. Learn from them. Find your role on the earth and carry it out selflessly, as do the earth, the sun and the moon. Believe in yourself. Walk out, walk alone, if necessary. *"Ekla chalo re,"* as the great Rabindranath Tagore advised.

We hate the sun in hot summer, only to love it again in cold winter. We are whimsical but our sun and earth are not. At times, we forget that the life on the earth is due to the sun. But the sun does not mind, it keeps burning alone, nonstop and keeps us warm and alive. It is only when our earth moves closer to the sun during a certain period of the year that we feel torched by it, and we curse it, as we curse everyone who has done something for us. We are ungrateful. The ladders that take us to the top are usually despised by us.

You don't matter to anyone except to yourself. Many great people have come here and gone. Many of them have been denigrated by many people long after they left. Don't expect anything from anyone. You are important to people only if and when you are seen as useful. If not, they will move on. That is life. No one will wait for you. Walk alone. *Ekla chalo re*!

As per the law of the universe, earth is destined to revolve around the sun, as moon is destined to revolve around the earth. But the earth is fair to all, it keeps rotating to expose everyone to the sun, causing day and night. Night refreshes us. You also find your destiny. You arrived here alone and alone you shall depart from here, and at any moment. That is the essence of life, transitory!

Ego usually wins against love, but it does not have to. Love expands and becomes inclusive, but ego contracts and becomes exclusive. Love is all about giving—a part of you and what you possess—unconditionally. Ego is about taking and possessing, selfishly. Love wins if it is pure. In love, your world is much beyond your personal self. With ego, however, your world shrinks and becomes much smaller than your heart.

Air and water are essential and vital for the survival of life. Both have no colour or odour in their natural state. Both look weak in terms of strength and are not even noticed. But when they move fast, with purpose and ferociously, they uproot and destroy everything in their path, without bias or discrimination. They can break and weather out the strongest of rocks and metals. Don't take them for granted. Similarly, never take a seemingly calm and gentle person for granted. Such a person is watching you silently. When this person rises, the world takes notice.

Suppose, one day, you find out that everything you knew about something, or were made to believe about some people or some issue was a well-crafted white lie. How would you turn back the clock and make amends? Consequences can be irreversibly hurting. Each one of us lives in several worlds. These include a personal world of our very own—as we see and feel—within and around us. In that world, we set our own laws, which others call our beliefs and superstitions. Strangely, these laws do work for and against us.

> *Live life fully to your very last moment till you fall down, dead. Life can be both like a whirlwind or a whirlpool—a burden or a breezy flight of joy—all depends on your hand of cards and how you play it. Spontaneity keeps it light and worth living. Live like a child. Learn from a child how to live.*

> *Don't think too deep into life, as it is much beyond you. An ocean can't be measured with a toothpick. Don't try to understand it with your head. Use and open your heart if you wish to live it well.*

Unhappiness

The world faces a significant challenge due to growing unhappiness and mental illness, especially of the youth, and even in older people, both in the developed world and the corresponding upper socio-economic strata in developing countries. One would intuitively assume that people who are materially rich and successful should be very happy. But are they?

In our quest to make things easier and our life relatively more comfortable, we distance ourselves from our *inner-self.* We have made ourselves more reliant, rather slavishly, on numerous external agencies for our happiness. Over time, due to a relatively more affluent lifestyle, as compared to that of our predecessors, we have become used to instant gratification of all our five senses, like instant noodles and tea bags! A famous cosmetic company keeps reminding us, *You are worth it*. Material consumption, eh! Furthermore, the availability of numerous options ruins us. We have forgotten those good old phrases—*all that glitters is not gold* and *appearances are deceptive*! Are we able to think? Do we have control on ourselves?

We feel lonely because we fail to connect with our inner-self. Accordingly, due to our internal vacuum, our lifestyle is driven, to a considerable extent, by the social media; we keep crying (albeit silently) '*look at me, look at me* ...' and suffer from an insatiable craving for maximum '*likes*' on social media. We are surely losing control on ourselves. Sadly, the locus of control is passed on and remains with others who decide how we should look, what we should wear, how we should live our life! Fashion industry and celebrities set the trends and most of us follow them—slavishly.

Through an aggressive advertisement campaign—overt and covert—subtle and bold—active and passive—material things and physical comforts are constantly being sold to us—right, left and centre—on both electronic and published media—on billboards, and by filthy rich and successful celebrities, who are paid truckloads of money to endorse and sell virtually everything to us (as if they were short of wealth, but human greed prevails). We are constantly being bombarded by the glitter; we keep getting lured into the (unhappy) material world. The more we move away from our inner-self, the unhappier we become. We are slowly but surely losing the necessary survival skills of deep contemplation, rationalisation and pure thinking in this ever-growing maze of material world.

A fast growing competition, due to uncontrolled population boom, and a constant struggle to survive, especially in a capitalistic world, keeps eroding our empathy and compassion for the fellow human being and the environment around us. It is mostly '*me, me, me*', just like lambs and sheep. We are proving we are nothing but another herd animal, but much more selfish, cunning and conniving. And also unhappy!

The want or absence of 'money' thwarts our dire need for spiritual satisfaction and internal dependence for happiness. Money has a limited influence—to the extent of our basic survival and does not impact our true happiness.

Being rich means giving away a part of your wealth or time to another person—materially poorer or wealthier—unconditionally, without any expectation—hidden or expressed—of a return.

An aimless life is similar to a piece of paper dropped from the top of a skyscraper, which drifts aimlessly, controlled only by wind and gravity. It may land on a lush green lawn or on a thorny rose bush, or even on a smoking rubbish dump or in an open stinking drain.

Don't let the clouds dampen your spirits ... transcend and cruise, the sun is always smiling above.

Mental Health

The world celebrates 10th October as the World Mental Health day. A consistent message from medical professionals, philosophers, people of wisdom and the religions, sums up the following 4-pronged approach to live a relatively more satisfied, balanced and fulfilled life:

- Live to an unselfish purpose of your choice;
- Unconditionally help others on a daily basis;
- Meditate daily; and
- Do some aerobic exercise regularly.

Mental health is not just about one day. This one day every year, 10th October, is just about promoting awareness about mental illness. Every day is actually a World Mental Health Day.(Anonymous)

It is okay not to be okay. Getting sick is normal! But it is never okay "not to do" something about it. Mental illness is just like any other sickness of any other body part. It is not madness. One must not follow any outdated taboos and stigmas about it. One in every four persons around us is known to have some form of mental illness; sadly, the number could be more than that.

Admit without shame that you are suffering. Discuss it with your family and friends, without hesitation or fear, that you have a problem. Seek the necessary medical help and get better. Give yourself time to heal and regain your mental health. As responsible adults, we are all responsible for looking after our mental health, as well as the health of our family members, work colleagues, friends and relatives. Let us do our bit. And, yes, let us not forget to breathe and be grateful that we are breathing.

As a child, in Kashmir, I played cricket outdoors in all seasons of the year. I played in the cold, rain, snow, mud and the sun. Life became much easier as I grew up. Those who stay outdoors and keep walking in the rain also happen to see a glorious rainbow after some time. Those who get drenched also relish a nice warm cup of tea.

“Life is a journey. Along the journey, we pick memories—good and bad, or both. Good memories are our only true treasures, while bad memories are just bags of toxic rubbish. At the end of the day, what does a person cherish—good memories or bad memories? Of course, the good memories, the true treasures! If we keep storing bad memories, we are certain to be sitting on a pile of toxic rubbish at the end of our life journey. It is, therefore, prudent to keep flushing all bad memories down the toilet as we keep going. For example, if anyone throws a bag of rubbish in your backyard, what do you do? You pick it up and throw it in a rubbish bin. You never take it inside your house. Similarly, bad memories must be rubbished and disposed off quickly. So the message is: Good memories must be treasured while bad memories must be laughed at." (Payam Sadeghi, 2019).

"Generally, people carry two suitcases all the time. One suitcase carries their past memories, of pain and suffering, losses and failures etc. The other suitcase carries their constant worries and apprehensions about their future, born out of fear (of imaginary failures) and anxiety (due to imagination of losing face and embarrassment). At any point of time, neither the past exists, nor is the future known! So, why do we keep carrying those two suitcases? Would it not be wise to travel light, without carrying those suitcases unnecessarily, and keep moving ahead happily through our life journey?" (George Cooper, 2019).

In 2019, I don't see many things the same way as I had seen them in 2018 or earlier. My perspectives on many things changed with time, in width and depth and, in some cases, in direction too. Thank God, my thoughts have not stagnated, I am truly alive. Life is movement and change is the only constant.

Both natural and engineered structures, like humans, have their individual 'ultimate' load capacities beyond which they collapse, or their deformation extends beyond their functional tolerance. A Factor of Safety is, therefore, used to limit their operational load and, therefore, deformation. Factor of Safety depends upon the importance and risk associated with the structure, as well as its nature and sensitivity. It is also dictated by the level of reliable information available in regard to the predictability of the behaviour of the structure. Like engineered structures, humans also need Factors of Safety, but at various levels of their existence—physical, mental, spiritual, financial, social etc.

> *How we respond, as pedestrians, to unexpected heavy downpours, defines our personality and how we meet sudden challenges in our lives. Rain tests our mental strength and determination to keep forging ahead, without stopping.*
>
> *When dark rain clouds are looming, or it is already pouring, it is no wisdom to hide indoors and wait, or pray like a coward, for clouds or rain to disappear. Instead, pick a good umbrella and / or wear a raincoat and bravely continue your normal life outdoors. Help yourself, it is no use just praying and wasting your time in hiding and doing nothing. As they say, "God helps those who help themselves."*

The New Year Myth

What changes between 31st December and 1st January? Absolutely nothing, zilch! Undoubtedly, the change in a calendar year is a strong reminder that we are left with lesser number of years before the end of our journey. So, what do we really celebrate on the eve of a new year? Do we celebrate the passing away of a (difficult?) year—i.e. lessening of the burden of life? Is living life so difficult? Or, do we celebrate a hope for a better year ahead? In essence, doesn't each morning give us a new lease of life? Shouldn't we celebrate each morning as soon as we realise that we are still alive to do things that we want to do?

Sun

Imagine, hypothetically, if there was only earth but no sun. It would be dark and extremely cold on earth, if at all it existed. There would be no photosynthesis and, therefore, no oxygen. So, would there be any life on the earth? Without the sun, there would be no solar system. All our planets, including earth, revolve around the sun, due to interplanetary gravitational forces. Would planets have existed without sun's gravity? Would Mother Earth really exist? Undoubtedly, as far as life is concerned, Mother Earth is equally responsible for its origin and survival on our planet.

How often do we humans thank the sun for what it does for us? We take everything as a matter of right but never think or fulfil our obligations. We are generally selfish, ungrateful and self-indulgent. All we think about is our own interest.

Sun is the reason for the creation and survival of life on our earth. Sun is our basic source of light and warmth. Sun warms our bodies, directly and indirectly through the food that we consume, which it helps to grow. Sun burns constantly for us all, selflessly. If the sun does not discriminate in giving us equally without bias, why do we discriminate against others based on how wealthy they are, how they look, what do they believe in, what do they do to earn their livelihood or where do they come from?

> *Sometimes, clouds hide the sun for many days. Those days look gloomy and things may look hopeless. But clouds are transient and shallow, and don't last long. They must disappear sooner or later to allow the sun to bathe everything in its warm, bright sunshine.*

Life

Life is a great leveller. Despite such a wide power differential across social hierarchy, it is only humbling, logical and just, and perhaps comforting for most, that the privileged, powerful and famous people in the world also breed, eat, walk, talk, cry and die just as their vastly underprivileged, much weaker and little known counterparts.

Life is as whimsical as weather. At times, when you don't carry an umbrella, it rains heavily or you need to walk in the hot sun. Sometimes, if you are lucky, unexpected help arrives. At most times, you are on your own. Luck is also whimsical. Live this moment. This moment alone is real. All other moments are either a memory or an imagination.

The future of life is life. A new start follows an end, as a day follows a night and spring follows winter. Change is the only constant. Destruction is usually followed by reconstruction, as peace follows war and hope follows despair. Life rocks us with the most unexpected shocks. The people you love the most, jolt you the most.

If life is divided into four stages, the first and the third stages are the most difficult. Extraordinarily brave are those people who keep fighting beyond their third stage. Most people just give up and wait for the inevitable after moving into their fourth stage, but only if they survive their third stage, and start preparing for the infinite beyond the imminent. Just wondering what could be a naturally dying person regretting not doing enough through his/her life?

Life presents an opportunity to each one of us to make a positive difference in this world, with ample reasons to make positive little changes in the lives of the people. Time and tide wait for none. Every breath I take is a gift from life. Let me live it well. Who knows if my gift lasts over the next minute or the next hour or the next day? Life is so unpredictable. It takes back everything that it gives. Empty-handed I arrived, empty-handed I shall depart. My bloody ego blinds me to this reality and the truth of life.

Without burning, you won't shine. Without pain, you won't shine. Without suffering, you won't shine. Without failing, you won't shine. Without falling, you won't rise. Has gold glittered without being melted? Does a diamond shine without being cut? Does the sun shine without burning? Does spring come before winter? Mothers endure pain when giving birth, a sign that pain is your best companion. It brings out the best from you. Nothing can be achieved or mastered without undergoing pain. No success comes without pain. So welcome pain.

Let the locus of our control be with us, within us. Let us learn to go within us sometime every day, stay there and enjoy ourselves. Count your blessings; you are alive and kicking to read this message. Keep breathing and be grateful.

This moment is like a passing wave, ride it or sink. You choose. Most of our life is much beyond our control; only a few fortunate ones reach their intended destination.

Resistance to change is an intrinsic part of the human nature. Newton's First Law of Motion (or Law of Inertia) supports this human tendency, but change is inevitable. Change is the only constant. But, as a wise person said, *"This will also pass."* Time and tide wait for none. Nothing is permanent. The unthinkable happens and takes one by surprise. Such things are called miracles. What looks unlikely happens. Sometimes, a certain victory suddenly turns into a defeat. *The Phoenix rises.* Wise never get carried away with petty victories. Middle path and sobriety are sustainable. Extremes collapse.

Intention to do good work may overlook the poor quality and inconsistency, but only to a minor extent. People must be held accountable for what they are paid to do. Your competition is not with anyone. Set your own milestones and keep going steadily, there is no rush. We are all moving in the same direction, believe it or not, and no one will be left behind. At the end, we pass on alone and empty-handed and it does not matter how much material wealth we have.

Movement is essential nature of life. Even when it may appear to stagnate, it keeps moving at subtle levels, which becomes perceivable after some time. Degradation of our bodies and materials by constant weathering and gravity reflects movement at micro levels.

In our solar system, all planets and moons keep moving all the time. The sun may appear to be stationary with respect to the planets but it too experiences significant thermal reactions within its body, which reflect in significant thermal activities on its surface. During severe storms, mainly the older branches of trees and plants, which are also bigger and stiffer than the younger branches, break and fall on the ground. The flexibility of younger branches allows them to bend, without cracking and falling off.

Always expect the unexpected. Dig in, come what may and never give up. Be flexible, resilient and tenacious to survive and win. If you are rigid, hard and brittle, you may get crushed under pressure.

Every journey has an end. Sadly, not all reach their destination at the end of their journey, some crash on the way and some realise they have just been chasing a mirage. Some accept the end-point as their destiny, and move on; some keep striving on. At conscious level, we may not realise it, but at our subconscious level, we are constantly seeking ourselves and our true nature. Somewhere, deep inside, we know we are our own best company. Don't we go quiet and seek within when we are distressed?

Most souls get derailed on the track of life. Only some souls become aware at some stage that they have derailed. Of those, only the brave manage to shake off their cloaks and succeed in returning to their natural state—naked and innocent, baby-like.

Today presents us with another opportunity to do what we want to do, read what we want to read, see what we want to see, go where we want to go and eat what we want to eat. Sadly, some of us earthlings may never have such an opportunity after today. Let us do today what is most important for us today. Tomorrow will take care of itself if we see it. It is always one step at a time.

There may not be one particular heaven or hell, there could be several and they should logically be here on this earth. Their descriptions in the traditional sense must be based on the human imagination, individual perspectives and one's state of mind. Heaven and hell must all be here. It is logically, rationally, scientifically and philosophically inconceivable that any heaven and hell could exist in the cosmos just for the departed souls. If we truly understand this reality, we will prevent ourselves from transforming virtual heavens on earth—as created by God or Nature—into hell.

One has to be truly blessed to be able to find some time on a regular basis and be able to contemplate about the nature of life itself after one's basics are covered. Material acquisitions won't bring any solace or comfort to us during our final moments, as they lose their relevance after a certain stage of life. It is only by gaining some understanding of the reality of life—and what possibly lies beyond—that makes any logical sense to fill our minds in the final stages of our life, i.e. what is it all about?

I am again falling in love with mountains. The hills and mountains humble me and win me over. They reflect stability and patience. Simply majestic! Mountains have a way of reminding one of one's roots. They reflect stability.

It is in man's conniving nature to get corrupted and corrupt others to own what he (she) wants to own. Formal education imparts sophistication and subtlety in corruption. Power and authority are its main drivers. Our wants and frailties sow its seeds.

Most of us, exercising a basic survival instinct, cling to the rays of hope and the possibilities of individual wins. We keep chasing happiness—in all its shapes and forms—through the satisfaction of all our five senses. Humans have learnt how to survive and look after their individual self. However, it is also true that our very tendency to chase happiness also thwarts our happiness. We keep looking for it outside of us--through the satisfaction of our five senses—without looking for it inside us.

With age, our thoughts become rigid and we begin to carry differing views from our mates that we have grown up with. Our disagreements lead to serious arguments at times. When heated arguments between partners and friends turn ugly, relationships break. One extreme gives birth to another extreme. For stability, it is best that one stays in the middle. Moderation and a middle path are the way to go.

The past does not exist. The present moment is the resultant and the sum total of all past moments. Only this moment is worth living. Sleeping in the past literally means missing the present. To keep glorifying the past means admitting current failures. Time flies and the opportunities pass by unharnessed; life goes backwards.

There are wishes, and wishes, and wishes—all noble wishes—all for us, our common good, oozing from every cell and sprouting as thoughts and blossoming as words—nothing but the noble wishes and prayers. But you always remain silent. You alone know when to strike and when to reward. You test our patience and faith, but why do you remain silent and invisible to the naked eye?

Going by Plato's 'cave analogy', a few 'free' souls, an extremely small percentage, who try to help millions of perpetual cave-dwellers to break free from darkness and see the light outside the cave, will not be trusted. They may even be attacked. As much as I trust the Higher Design, I don't want to relieve humans of their responsibility and the accountability for their actions and inactions. We must not leave things to God if we are able to do them. Let us do our bit and let God keep our earth safe and complete and let the sun keep us warm and bright. Together we achieve common good. Stay close, together. Nothing much can be achieved otherwise.

How unethical it is to take credit for someone else's good work or kind gesture? Give the credit where it rightfully belongs.

Your health and time are your greatest assets. Invest them wisely.

Namaskar—with both hands folded and pointing upwards—depicts the omnipresence of God, i.e. God resides within everything and everyone. If you use this greeting, you must not abuse or disrespect anyone, as that would be disrespectful to God and construed as blasphemous.

I have a dream and I do believe in miracles and angels. Importantly, I also believe in myself and the difficult, yet noble path I am treading to stitch this world together. Indians generally show a tendency to dig into sensational stories and conspiracies of the past. They don't really think much about their present and the future. Perhaps reading stories is much more engaging than thinking about issues and their solutions.

How you address and treat the people you dislike defines you. People who are self-respecting show respect towards others too. All humans carry intrinsic dignity, which must be respected. One does not look after people by creating new and / or nurturing existing barriers between people; one looks after them by removing all barriers and looking after them with equal care.

Verily, we turn a full circle. Our past, like gravity, is pulling us back. We romanticised about the past and never learnt to break free and live in the future. We closed our eyes to the reality and retreated to tread a familiar path. Tears may roll down now, but to what use? What falls seldom rises again.

It took us thousands of years to reach this point, but it may not take much time to go back to the caves. How foolishly we let our vanity murder our future! None can save us if we choose pride over wisdom. How can we ever cruise if our wings are fettered by the chains of the past? India, it is time to look over the Himalayas.

God's creation is perfect. Sun gives us light and warmth; oceans give us water and food; and earth gives us birth, food and resources.

We are always wrong in judging others if we are not perfect ourselves. As fools, we cast aspersions about people we have never met or interacted with. If they don't know us, they don't give a damn what we think about them. Our negative thoughts—fear, jealousy and hate—about others pollute our mind and exacerbate our imperfections further, and we keep falling. We become spiritually unhealthy. If our measuring yardstick is imperfect, varying, and whimsical and subject to moon and the tidal influences, or influenced by greed, temptations or fear—our assessment is wrong and invalid.

When everything looks dark and cloudy, a bright patch of sky appears at the horizon, signalling hope and calling for optimism.

The past thousands of years have made us chronically poor, despite our current newfound wealth, and perpetually insecure. Characteristically, we sacrifice the other person when we feel insecure or if our interest is under threat. Generally, we use our authority and wealth power to fleece the other person. However, with people of equal status, we tend to use the subtle weapon of show-off to implode and burn them with jealousy and envy.

What is lost is lost, no use crying over the spilt milk. We have to be pragmatic and focus on the present and wisely shape up our future. Our future is in our hands. It is imprudent to remain buried in the past, irrespective of how glorious or gloomy was that past? Life moves forward and not backward.

The economists have distorted and corrupted our thoughts. Economic growth rate mainly reflects human greed and material consumption, but does not reflect human happiness, health and wellbeing. Never judge a country by only its economic growth rate. Social structure resembles a pyramid. The number of your companions and your visibility depend on your position in the pyramid. As you rise in the pyramid, your visibility increases but the number of your companions falls. It is a very lonely world at the top of the pyramid; you pay a heavy price for your visibility Mutual trust, care and compassion are the founding blocks and binding fabric of a community. If one distrusts more than 50 percent people that one knows from one's community, such a community will inevitably fall and disintegrate. We live in very strange times. Whilst it is increasingly becoming more and more difficult, rather practically impossible, to verify the integrity of any person or the authenticity of any news report, our tolerance and respect for the other person has also sadly dwindled.

As per natural law, the rich and the fit survive whereas the weak and the poor perish. Materialism and capitalism live this law, but benevolent governments and caring families defy this law.

They made their children timid every time they scared away their young children from saying or doing certain things: "Don't do it, otherwise 'koukha' will come!" This 'koukha' was an imaginary demon. Those children grew up timid.

Thinking used to make a clear difference between the humans and the other species. Things changed as their numbers grew, they became more intelligent but much less wiser. How often do we think about the pain that produces music? That flute which has holes carved out and that string in the musical instrument which is constantly tensioned. The gold that we see glitter has undergone the hell of heat and pounding; the diamond that shines has been cut and cut and cut by its jeweller. A rainbow only appears after therain. Spring only arrives after rain. Our heart deepens with grief and suffering till we sing poetry. That nightingale knows what it took to produce her music.

Any situation or a person, that you try to escape from, will keep confronting you till you don't hold the bull by its horns. Face your adversaries head on, don't escape, don't abdicate. For Heaven's sake, don't let your life be controlled or misused or abused by anyone. You owe your life and body to your parents and their persistent hard work. It is your prime responsibility to take good care of your body and soul. After your parents, you are your own caretaker, your own little god. Be your own boss. Don't give in, don't give up. Run with your life and win.

By calling a spade a spade, you remove the masks as truth is bitter. People will not like you. They apply make-up and deodorant to hide. Have the courage to question the accuracy, validity, authenticity and integrity of everything that is being fed to you without any evidence.

Our own teeth sometime bite our tongue. (Anonymous, a Chinese saying). "We despise the stairs that lead us to the top" my worthy grandfather would often quote, perhaps from an English play, when I was a child. Over time, as I grew, I realised its validity in our social and political world.

Most people in the world worry about their next meal and the remaining burn their energy in showing off their wealth to the next person. The world's 1% population owns more than 50% wealth. In India, possibly the top 20% own 80% or more of the country's wealth.

Many lions and tigers roar in the jungle of social media. Some wolves howl and some elephants trumpet. Some birds make beautiful music. Snakes and lizards slither quietly and creepy crawlies remain hidden. Human behaviour is not different to other herds. Their behaviour turns 180 degrees when they move from a minority community to a majority community. Our nose depicts human mortality. Humans need it to breathe, to stay alive. Immortals don't need it. It also represents human pride. It keeps growing in size with age. Look after your nose.

It is not really important how old you are; what is important is how much life you are left with. More importantly, how do you live it from now on? As providence wills, we find ourselves in this situation. Now how we deal with it is a matter of our choice. Christians celebrate the life of the departed on the day of the funeral. Hindus cry and wail. Destiny can't be changed. We have been used by our destinies as actors.

I am striving along ... hoping someone listens ... hoping some magic happens ... it is risky and may cost me my life one day. But that is fine, as long as it brings about some positive changes. My personal struggles become insignificant when I recall those 1 billion underprivileged people, their faces and their daily struggles. In their desperation they pray to God! Don't they?

It is not always very easy to follow the middle-of-the-road approach, as people doubt and target you. Most people believe if you don't parrot them, you are acting against them. Your personal risk increases significantly if some of them 'claim' to be nationalists, in which case you can be labelled as an anti-national element. Follow your lane and don't disrupt others. All lanes lead you in the same direction. Take care of your safety and the safety of your fellow commuters.

Herd mentality! In my younger days, I would hear my elders saying, "Individually, people are very good but their behaviour and attitude changes completely in a mob." As a grown-up, I can now relate to what they would say. I hear many people in private rubbishing everything and criticising every Tom, Dick and Harry—left, right and centre. However, I get quite puzzled to read their posts on social media. Herd mentality, I reckon. People fear social retribution. They want to be visible but fear getting identified for expressing any unpopular views. Their safest (and wisest) approach is to move with the wind.

Life without humour is like a day without sunshine, or an ice-cream without sugar, or chips without salt. Learn to laugh at yourself too!

Stick to the austere all-weather constant and not the flashy seasonal variables. They are like patches of drifting clouds, won't give you shade when you need it.

One day when we are old and feeble, without our current good looks or charms, we'll face our conscience. Even memory loss and Alzheimer's disease won't help. We will rue many of our present decisions and actions. Our conscience will be our greatest tormentor.

Your present moment is shaping your future. Live it wisely and don't blame your destiny or luck. If you are able to digest your food and sleep soundly during night, you are one of the most fortunate people in the world. No one is too beautiful or perfect not to be judged just ordinary. Beauty lies in the eyes of the beholder. Those who judge others also risk being judged. However, only those people matter who actually act. The sun will shine and the earth will move every day; workers don't stop, rain or shine.

Alone we arrive, alone we depart. We may meet and travel with many individuals like us along the way but our journey remains solely our own. At the end, we are left alone to reconcile our successes with our failures. We are accountable only to ourselves.

Life presents itself in infinite shades,with or without cosmetics. From time to time, nature reveals its true face, raw and without cosmetics—that humbles the bravest of mortals. Civilisations come and go. Dust returns to dust and bubbles explode. Silence returns.

A philosopher is a soul stirrer, one who constantly endeavours to use reason and logic to seek the truth, keeps nudging himself and others to face oneself and one's conscience.

When truth starts to shiver and tremble, a natural upheaval is imminent, as the world moves into an unstable equilibrium. It is important, therefore, for the soldiers of truth to tread fearlessly.

Life springs pleasant surprises when one expects them the least. After dark stormy hours, beautiful rainbows appear when the sun shines.

Impermanence is the essence of life. Life is temperamental and whimsical. Fools take it for granted.

Wisdom

Wisdom and intelligence are two different terms, with two different meanings. They may commonly be confused as having the same meaning. Wisdom can't be bought by money or stolen from books. It is a gift from nature. Only some fortunate souls are born with it. It allows them to see much beyond intelligence, higher from logic and deeper than knowledge.

It is wisdom that sets apart an illiterate wise person from an intelligent fool. The former can look much beyond and wider than the latter. Wisdom transcends education and knowledge. It envisions the wise to peep into the unknown whereas the educated remain limited within the bounds of knowledge. Wisdom is the core characteristic of visionaries. Amongst the educated, only a few are wise. Wisdom and intelligence may not always marry each other. One can be patient and farsighted and the other impatient and short-sighted.

Students of life may also acquire some wisdom after going through the grind of life. Their life experience teaches them about the real facets of life that books don't teach. *The human mind invents reasons to trick it in believing in and justifying ethically wrong things. All for survival and just like other herd animals. Humans are our greatest source of joy; and also our greatest source of sorrow. Choose your friends wisely. It is extremely humbling to realise that a human, if immortal, will possibly take hundreds of lifetimes to fully understand how the world runs, or perhaps never. Not surprising, humans are so very imperfect. Only fools can call themselves gods or world experts.*

Intellectual hierarchical structure resembles a pyramid or a trapezoidal prism structure. You have the company of only a few in the upper part of the structure. Your wealth or position don't set you apart from others, your intellectual wisdom does. As your vision widens, your horizon enlarges. You rise above the crowd, when your thoughts are noble and contrastingly differ from the masses. You are alone, but never lonely. Nature will nourish you. *When you are alone, you have the opportunity to enjoy your own company and energise yourself, you are close to Nature. But when you feel lonely, you are disconnected from yourself and Nature.*

> *Verily this moment—like any other past or future moment—will roll into oblivion. It will matter and be remembered, by you or by others, only if you capture it and shape it in your uniquely own meaningful, documented thought or action. Nothing matters in the end. We become a story but only if our actions make a story.*
>
> *Between wisdom and intelligence, the former invariably wins and becomes a saviour.*

Lies

Lies don't fly very far. Lies are little birds that fly with wings of wax. Truth melts them down sooner or later, leading to their fall. The bigger the lie and the higher it flies, the louder and more spectacular is its crash. Fasten your belt and enjoy the flight. Truth never dies. It hibernates in every cell of ours—in the deepest nooks and corners of our conscience.

We all know what the truth is and what a lie is. Truth lives within each one of us; it always comes out. In some cultures, however, truth may take a little more time to come out. Nature has universal laws—for everyone and for all places.

A liar always knows the truth and can't escape. A liar may tell a thousand lies to suppress it but it will always emerge. A liar may deceive the whole world but not oneself. As long as there is one living person who knows the truth, God knows it. It will come out any moment. And that one person could even be the liar himself.

> *A lie told consistently may assume the adornment of a fake reality. But the truth will always emerge and burn down its false facade, exposing it shamefully, stark naked.*

Divide & Rule

In Kashmir, every street, *mohalla*, suburb and village had its own unique culture. Despite cultural differences, Kashmir has remained as one single entity. For that matter, Jammu and Kashmir are two entirely different places in terms of their cultures, climate and languages but even then, they have remained as the two essential parts of one single state. It puzzles me how the partition of India was allowed to happen in 1947, considering more Muslims remained with India than those who went to Pakistan.

As if that is not surprising enough, the separation of East Pakistan from West Pakistan, which gave birth to Bangladesh, in 1971, is a big puzzle. In the recent years, India has been seeing the birth of a number of new states, and more new states may be in the offing. Families get divided as the smallest units of any community.

Affluent Kashmiri people generally follow a more materialistic, capitalistic lifestyle, as seen from their behaviour and showy rituals and ceremonies. This marks a major shift in their mentality, from spiritual to material. Kashmiri Pandits copied this behaviour from other (host) cultures in India. It is like a petrol engine being run on diesel. It will undoubtedly undermine their identity and culture unless they restore a balance between a materialistic and a spiritual lifestyle.

Kashmiri Pandits are obligated to look after what they have been known for and not try to acquire any new identity. Their most important asset used to be their ability to think, and their wisdom and intelligence. Their balanced lifestyle always aimed for stability, sustainability and togetherness.

A vibrant Kashmir could make the whole subcontinent vibrant, whereas a sick Kashmir will potentially make it sicker. Kashmir—the geographical and spiritual head of the subcontinent is the key to peace in the region. Patriotic Kashmiri Pandits have an important role to play, as Kashmir will eventually decide the destiny of the subcontinent.

Leaders differ from managers. Leaders lead, while managers manage. Leaders work as part of their team, while managers tend to boss their team. Leaders blame themselves but credit others; however, managers blame others but credit themselves.

It is always important to know the core reasons 'why' certain unfortunate things have happened, especially if they have resulted in significant human loss, pain and suffering, then reflect on them with an open and calm mind, and finally help to implement the necessary measures to prevent recurrences.

Many people work mainly to make their ends meet but don't actually love the work they do 8 am to 6 pm. Those who do love their work do it regardless and don't greatly care if they are paid well or not. To 'work for one's passion' and to have 'passion for one's work' are two different things. Happiness and fulfilment issues arise when they are confused with each other. As a result, the people's mental health and the quality of work suffer. The nation suffers.

You are never alone. There is no place where you can hide, so stop escaping or hiding. Your memory of yourself is evidence you are being watched and recorded constantly.

It is not the religion or the culture which may be causing separations. It is possibly the greed and the lust for power that divides. People divide countries and states to acquire power. They continue to divide the people to stay in power. Human greed, and not religion or culture, is thus the cause of human suffering. It will always remain so.

Faith and Religion

All lanes lead to the same destination. There may be dashed lines or bold lines between the lanes, but as long as we stay within a lane and not interfere with other commuters, we'll reach there safely. Let us respect the safety of commuters in other lanes too. Belief--systems, religious faiths and philosophies also lead to the same end-point. We live and die in the same one world.

Hinduism is a way of life, a philosophy but not a religion. It is like an ocean—all accommodating, all inclusive—and not limited like a river. There is no one book in Hinduism and there are no strict or regimented dos and don'ts. Sadly, some so called Hindus, who don't know what it means to be a Hindu, misinterpret the philosophy and practice it as if it was a religion. My grandfather used to say, *"If you have self-respect and love your religious faith, you must then respect others too and their faith. Treat them as you wish to be treated by them."*

Diwali, the Festival of Lights, signifies goodness, peace and prosperity. It is all about giving away our best. Let us radiate goodness and spread smiles this day and every day.

In the course of our life journey, our minds get shaped and chiselled by our self-learning and experiences, as rocks get rounded off by physical weathering caused by water and wind. Most changes in us happen at very subtle levels, which our conscious mind does not readily decipher or see. Not many people are able to perceive changes in themselves. That is why it is necessary that one gets appraised by others. But if others also change as we change, we won't be able to correctly measure the changes in us. All changes are relative to fixed benchmarks. Using that analogy, if we all are moving in the same direction and at the same speed, we are relatively stationary with respect to one another.

I am a born Hindu—a Saraswat Brahman—from Kashmir. I am entitled to use the title 'Pandit' before my name. But I am not sure if I am truly a Pandit in a traditional sense. I see a Pandit in every human who functions as a Pandit in a traditional sense. These titles, categories and castes are meaningless in this day and age. The attritions of my life have undoubtedly rounded off my angularities. My practices of meditation and deep contemplation have metamorphosed me from a more ritualistic Hindu to a more spiritualist Hindu.

I could also use my other analogy, of a river and an ocean. Most of my ritualistic Hindu relatives call me an atheist, just because I meditate but not perform rituals. I just smile back. When I ask them some basic questions—as I am a seeker—they feel offended and they have no answers. Some of them remind me of people from other relatively more rigid faiths.

I am a vegetarian since my childhood and I strive constantly for peace and harmony with nature, and that includes our fellow humans. I can't understand how and why some people advocate violent solutions to solve violent issues. For me, all humans and animals are sacred.

Remain sincere and steadfast in your noble endeavours. Your resolution will be tested. Don't give in, don't give up. When can we dare to see what we have been avoiding to see? Nature is looking at us through the eyes of all people around us; there is no escape.

Ostrich attitude means burying one's head in the sand, in an attempt to refuse to see/admit the reality. When the ostrich buries its head in sand, the hunter easily gets hold of it. Similarly, when people refuse to see the reality by fooling themselves or through self-hypnosis they soon fall prey and get consumed quickly. For some lucky ones, however, ignorance may sometimes be bliss but only till the hunter reaches and grabs their neck.

Short fuses undermine peace in the families and the country.

Your self-control defines peace in your life. Don't let others agitate you to the point of your explosion. Keep your powder dry. No one knows tomorrow, so it may be reasonable to an extent, if at all, to worry about it and how it unfolds, given the uncertain and whimsical nature of life. But it is baffling to note why people brood and fight over their past which is known in different shades to different people but does not exist anymore.

While people brood and fight for the past, they miss living in the present moment, which provides one with the only opportunity to improve one's life. Thus, their past not only ruins their present, it also becomes the bad seed of their future, without causing any improvement in their lives. With age, our thoughts become rigid and we begin to carry differing views from our mates whom we have grown up with. Our disagreements lead to serious arguments at times. When heated arguments between partners and friends turn ugly, relationships break.

> *Rivers run to meet and merge with oceans and oceans accommodate them. A river may fight with an ocean but how silly would it be for an ocean to fight with a river.*
>
> *Paint your own canvas. Chose a direction and keep moving. There will be many obstacles in the way but you will prevail if your focus is strong, intent, sincere, objective and unselfish. Be resilient and tenacious, so you won't break. Bruised and battered you may become but, undoubtedly, you will reach there.*

Home and Belonging

If an unresolved issue of the past has the potential to become a seed of death and destruction in the future, it must be extracted with extreme care and caution, and defused safely in the same manner as a buried bomb is extracted and defused by experts.

We are constantly being fed with seemingly *credible and believable* information through commercial, medical, religious and political propaganda channels. Not many can practically verify if such information is really genuine. Some do but not before it is too late. *Sometimes, it is much wiser and safer to leave a bullet inside the body than run a risk in removing it. Some tricky past issues are best left untouched. Why muddy the waters by scratching the river bed? It is not always advisable to uncover buried mess or open a can of worms. Let the genie sleep undisturbed.*

Do we have any other option than following the path of positivity? Imagine Nature being negative, the world would not exist. If one follows Nature, one follows positivity. Natures nurtures, nourishes and provides. My esteemed teacher once advised, *"Even in your dreams, you must not think negative. You are gifted with power to change the world for the better. Have faith in yourself and keep pushing ahead with only positive thoughts and positive actions."*

I was blinded when I was there. I was too close to see the reality. From afar, I have been able to see it. Distance and detachment are essential for clarity. My soil lives 12,000 km away from its mother land, but my soul lives where my soil was born. Mother keeps calling.

Sadly, many of us lacked (and still do) a sense of belonging to Kashmir; some looked to the west and some to the south of our homeland. We, all Kashmiris, must earnestly connect with our roots and one another, and rediscover ourselves. Cultural scour and spiritual erosion—and not physical displacement—mark the demise of a community. The day all Kashmiris—Pandits and Muslims—take pride in being Kashmiris, accept and love their roots, a new Kashmir will be born.

Verily, through science, literature, philosophy and contemplation, we seek what we are born to seek. But only when we truly surrender, the Truth is revealed. Our inward and outward eyes open at our surrender. New wealth and new power show on the surface of a person. Many people can't easily control them and usually lose their mental equilibrium. The mentality and behaviour of such intoxicated people represents the actual inner person, who is still poor and insecure.

He was expected to heal, bind, integrate and secure but, sadly, he ended up doing the opposite. He was everywhere but not there. He spread himself thin. He brought in hope but left behind despair. History, you don't miss anything.

Accept and respect your neighbour whosoever he or she may be. If not, please move and never poison your mind with hatred or fear.

Unless a tree has deep roots, for strength and nourishment, it can't grow tall and bear fruit. Similarly, a tall building needs deep foundations for stability. Likewise, a tall leader must be deeply knowledgeable and caring, like a mother.

Someone must keep their eyes open. Someone must think deeply. Someone must care. You be that someone. It does not matter how many innings you have played. it is a new start each time. Play each inning well, with heart. You will be tested and teased. Play patiently and weather out all tests. You will reach your goal.

Liberalism must never be taken for weakness. Like air and water, liberals are peaceful and normally relaxed, but their behaviour changes completely when they are abused and challenged. On the other hand, extremism may appear to be hard, but it is quite brittle. It breaks easily due to lack of elasticity, flexibility, tenacity and resilience.

We are all on a slippery slope, so respect your elders! It may be understandable why young people in their twenties criticise and make fun of people in their fifties, but it baffles me how the people in their fifties also do the same to the older people in their seventies and eighties.

> *I must keep walking whether you walk with me or not. I must walk for you and me. Right now, you may be half asleep, half intoxicated, half dreaming, half drowsy, half euphoric and half hallucinating. I must try to secure you for yourself, so that you can find yourself when you wake up one day and look for yourself.*

Strength

Strength does not mean having to boisterously announce to the world how strong you are. It does not mean disrespectfully shouting loudly at your adversaries, threatening them and telling them how weak or poor they are, or how they will lose the fight if they fight you. Strong people know they are strong, they don't feel the need to show their strength to scare weaker and poorer people. They don't abuse their strength. They help the weak and the poor, using humane ways, and not by force. They use their strength for the good of other people. Strong people are not paranoid about their adversaries. Paranoia about ones adversaries reflects ones weakness and not strength.

> *Deep rivers don't roar, they move silently and nourish millions, they are strong. Shallow rivers just roar. Trees laden with ripe fruit stand humble—with their fruit bearing branches bending low—and not proud. Cockiness reflects hollowness and arrogance.*

Suffering

Sufferer suffers, sufferer knows, sufferer remembers. Suffering returns to the ones who cause suffering in much greater measures. The longer it takes to return, the bigger is the suffering. Sufferer alone knows where it pinches. What insensitive bystanders think does not matter, it is not their suffering. For most, it is a show. Sadistic bystanders derive pleasure from watching the sufferer wriggle with pain.

Time witnesses and remembers everything, time remembers suffering. Suffering lives forever in the memory of sufferers and those who love them. Suffering is a seed that time nurtures, as a baby is nurtured by its mother. Seeds of suffering give birth to thorny plants of suffering that grow into large, monstrous trees of suffering, which deliver bitter fruits of suffering. When nurtured by hate, vengeance or retribution, seeds of suffering also give birth to destructive demons and monsters of doom. Healing balms, applied to sufferers with sincere care, empathy and love, prevents the trees, demons and monsters of greater suffering from taking birth.

Those who nurture the seeds of retribution and revenge, for whatever reason, legitimate or not, actually nurture the seeds of doom and death. They get imprisoned in a perpetual cycle of suffering. Their liberation lies only in their forgiveness of their adversaries.

One who derives pleasure in the suffering of another person, one's adversary or otherwise, has fallen spiritually. One who justifies such pleasure has fallen morally and ethically. And one who legitimises this suffering has fallen as a human.

Freedom

Who is free? What is freedom? Where is freedom? How many of us are absolutely free—from the controls and clutches of our parents, relatives (eg in-laws), life partners, community and community leaders, religion and religious leaders, teachers, employers, government, and the law & order? How many of us are prepared to give absolute freedom to our children, life partners, students and employees?

While we remain entrapped in the tunnels of our mind, the sun keeps shining. Break free and bathe yourself in the sunshine before the sun sets. No material in the world can buy the experience of freedom—the absolute freedom, when you are your own master and you are your own slave. It is a divine, exhilarating feeling much beyond any human imagination. Paint your own canvas. Chose a direction and keep moving. There will be many obstacles in the way but you will prevail if your focus is strong, intent, sincere, objective and unselfish. Be resilient and tenacious, so you won't break. Bruised and battered you may become but you will complete your canvas one day.

Freedom is our ultimate birthright. Your freedom lies in my freedom. When I become free, you too naturally become free. Let us help each other in setting ourselves free. We are precariously leaning on each other and making our lives difficult. While you crave for your victory, I crave for my freedom. My victory lies in my freedom but your victory lies in taking away my freedom.

Freedom comes with self-restraint, discipline, citizenship, responsibility and accountability. One must pay the price for infringing on the rights and dignity of others. Trespassing must be punishable.

When we live in a particular system, we become enslaved to others and, as such, the system itself, to a lesser or a greater degree. We enslave and we are enslaved. An educated, clever, powerful bureaucrat also salutes and serves an uneducated or semi-educated but powerful politician. We enslave some people and some other people enslave us. A bigger fish eats the smaller fish.

Freedom is a relative state of mind and the web of materialism is our prison. Absolute freedom is a myth and possibly perhaps comes only with death, or perhaps not. In relative terms, the degree of freedom increases as our wants and material needs decrease.

Freedom is the ultimate goal of life. Living a long life but without much freedom is like a random leaf that flies around aimlessly. Your freedom is your obligation to yourself. You were born to attain it. Your freedom from yourself is the highest gift that you can ever give to yourself. No one will ever give it to you except you, yourself. Unchain your fetters. You have to figure out yourself how to do that.

Since the time you starting thinking and moving after your birth, you weaved a web of your likes and dislikes around you, which trapped you within your own mind. You enslaved yourself. Your attachments to your likes imprisoned you.

So did your dislikes and hates. Accept the world around you as it is and transcend to freedom. You fell to numerous temptations of this world, not realising you were chasing illusions. You walked into a perpetual prison through your five senses. You will never be free till you don't detach yourself from the material world around you and purge yourself of materialism, which has encapsulated your spirit. Set your spirit free.

A slave is not one who is physically chained by others but one who does not have much freedom to exercise one's will. There is no bigger hell than slavery. Death provides dignified freedom when all other options to be free look impossible.

Exercise freedom responsibly. More often than not, we say or do whatever we please or feel like, without considering the consequences of our actions. We believe, as we are free, we have the entitlement (from God) to show our autonomy and a 'devil-may-care' attitude. As such, we go by a mindset that the onus is always on the other people, how they take it and respond.

Only a truly free person can value and respect another person's freedom. As we truly don't understand and appreciate the meaning of freedom and, therefore, don't exercise the responsibility that comes with it, our freedom may not last long. There is always someone more powerful to snatch it away from us.

It does not matter much how others see you or what they think about you. What matters more is how you see yourself and if you respect yourself. Your human progress is defined by the degree of independence and purity in your thought and action, and the extent to which your life is in your control. There is no bigger jail than being imprisoned by your superstitions and beliefs.

Your true wealth is your health and personal dignity. If you are not able to enjoy your company, you will always be at the mercy of others. Sooner or later, you will lose yourself. If your wealth and power are not able to bring you internal peace, you have wasted your life. Only when you are able to find peace in yourself, you will be at peace with the world around you. Your internal chaos will manifest in more chaos around you. Fortunate are those who are in control of their body and mind. Human progress manifests in simplicity of thought and a reduction in material needs.

A rash, rowdy and bullying behaviour exhibited by the drivers of expensive cars on the roads is a classic illustration of a snobbish, arrogant mindset. Your road behaviour defines you.

There are occasions when we wish the traffic light never turns green, or the train runs slower or the plane keeps flying eternally. And there are occasions when we wish hours, days, months and years pass in a jiffy. Similarly, sometimes we wish our dream was real and the real life just a nightmare. Life reveals its strange, paradoxical shades of different colours from time to time.

Earth can't keep up with the whimsical nature of the human mind. It can't slow down or move faster just because we wish so from time to time. Time has its own pace but our mind keeps varying its pace. No human is more privileged and as resourceful or powerful than life and nature. Humans must realise this reality before they bite the dust. No one knows tomorrow, so it may be reasonable to an extent, if at all, to worry about it and how it unfolds, given the uncertain and whimsical nature of life. But it is baffling to note why people brood and fight over their past—which is known in different shades to different people—but does not exist anymore.

While people brood and fight for the past, they miss living in the present moment, which provides one with the only opportunity to improve one's life. Thus their past not only ruins their present, it also becomes the bad seed for their future, without causing any improvement in their lives.

When nothing is visible and life become very uncertain, trust your heart and the ground that you are standing upon; don't move till your visibility improves. A single step could land you in abyss. Don't chase illusions unless they prove to be real. Your past is dead and buried; never bury yourself in your past. Your present is the net resultant of your past; your present is real and your life is in the present.

If only we could realise how extremely fortunate we are—to be in that exclusive and privileged club of the world's top two-percent population, which is educated and relatively affluent—we would be extremely humble and grateful. We could have been born in a poor community of a poor country, or in a slum-dwelling anywhere on this planet. It is not really important how old you are; what is important how much life you are left with. More importantly, how do you live it from now on? At hard and difficult times, when you become aware about your insignificance and feel overwhelmed by ferocious elements, it is prudent that you lie low till your adversary weakens or moves on, otherwise you will be crushed or blown away.

Patience and prudence are your best friends. Nourish these virtues through respect and nurture them by practice. Being aware about your limitations and knowing the time when you should quit are keys to your survival. Life can always offer you numerous opportunities to bounce back and at the right time but, till then, just become invisible.

When lies are convincingly and artfully used by powerful or influential people with innocent looks and good acting skills, to malign and accuse their intended victims, without receiving any effective rebuttal and resistance in return from any person, they become reality. The truth takes a long time to emerge but not before the victims suffer immense personal loss of reputation and damage to their life and credibility. In many such cases, justice is never delivered.

Believe in yourself and trust yourself. Walk out, walk alone, if necessary. *Ekla chalo re,* as the great Tagore advised. You arrived here alone and alone you shall depart from here, and at any moment. That is life. You don't matter to anyone except to yourself. Many greats have come and gone. Many of them have been denigrated by people long after they left. Don't expect anything from anyone. You are important to people only if and when you are seen as useful. If not, they will move on. That is life. No one will wait for you. Walk alone.

With so much negativity, hate and fear in the air, the only thing that can save us and our children are our positive thoughts, which we must sow as seeds for reaping positive fruits, and follow up with sincere actions. There are numerous diseases and human challenges in the world but those millions of scientists, doctors, engineers, academics and philosophers don't give up their fight to overcome them. Thanks to those mad dreamers, the world of 2019 is not the same as the world of 1819.

I deliberately close my eyes for a few moments every day and drift back into the days of my childhood. I imagine the presence of my elders and many warm and caring relatives, friends and neighbours, soak in their love and care, and then return to the present.

> *We give what we have, we give what we receive. We can, however, choose to absorb the bitterness and regurgitate only the good, so as to break the cycle of karma.*
>
> *When dark clouds look threatening and wind blows hard, a storm may be imminent. It is no wisdom to be optimistic and stay in the open. And it is no bravery to challenge nature and not take shelter in time.*

> *Freedom is only an internal state of mind. Only a few attain it. External freedom is just a myth. So is 'independence'—be it political, economic or personal.*
>
> *Home is where I live; home is where my fellow humans live. The whole world is my home.*

Language

A culture can survive only if its language and literature are able to survive the challenges of time, which depends on whether or not it is proactively nourished by the community. Food, clothing and spirituality are also important but serve only as the supporting factors for its preservation. Preserve your language to preserve your culture and community. You may speak a hundred languages but your cultural identity will be rooted mostly in your mother tongue. You mother tongue will nourish your spirit. Except your mother tongue, no other language shall be able to convey your expressions of love to your beloved, faith to your god and sincerity to your friend without undergoing distortion and adulteration.

> *Language is the heart and soul of a culture. A community that replaces the language and, thus, the culture of its ancestors—knowingly or unknowingly, deliberately or inadvertently—with languages (and, thus, the cultures) of its neighbouring communities is deemed to have truly uprooted and orphaned itself. Such a community is well and truly in the process of irreversible permanent decay.*

Bide Your Time, O Little Old Bird

It is so cold, wet and windy out there; you will be blown away.
Bide your time, O little old bird, bide your time.
You have flown so long; you have flown so high, you are run down.
Bide your time, O little old bird, please bide your time.
Let the gentle warm sun appear and let the wind turn into a caressing breeze.
Bide your time, O little old bird, bide your time.
Save your breath for the longest flight of your life for which you need to soar high.
Bide your time, O little bird, bide your time.
Remember those mesmerising moments when you soared high in that deep blue sky.
Bide your time, O little bird, bide your time.
On your longest flight, you will soar so high that the earth will appear so sublime.
Bide your time, O little old bird, bide your time.
Keep resting and dreaming in your little nest till the time is right for you to fly again.
Bide your time, O little old bird, bide your time.

All paths lead to the same destination

Be stable like the mountains

THREE

SPIRITUALITY IN LIFE

Heaven & Hell

HEAVEN AND HELL are here and now, both within us. When we are at peace with ourselves, we are in heaven. In our peaceful state of mind, we radiate peace and we live in harmony with the other living beings. We remain settled and we are more accommodating and forgiving. Most importantly, we remain civil. We cherish and show respect for the inherent human dignity. When we are unhappy inside, we tend to be angry and radiate anger. Anger consumes us.

We live with an unsettled state of mind and remain reactive; people run away from us. Our unsettled mind also tries to unsettle the world around us. In that state of mind, we also lose civility and respect for the inherent human dignity. Our thoughts become muddled. Fear and insecurity, real or unreal—are generally the basic reasons underlying unhappiness. Many people get caught in paranoia. Everything looks pale to a jaundiced eye. One thing leads to another, there is no end!

Blind people (due to ignorance and not physical blindness) quarrel with one another about the shape of the elephant. The world is not so black and white; most of it is in different shades of grey. Unfortunately, people who see the world only in black and white invariably cause strife in their own lives and in the lives of others.

To err is human and to forgive divine. Without knowing the truth, the whole truth, absolutely, one must never pass judgement. If God judged us, bad people would have no access to air, water and food. If we respect ourself, we'll respect others too. If we respect our parents, we'll respect the parents of other people too. If we respect our thoughts and opinions, we must respect the opinions and thoughts of others too. Our karma will catch up with us one day, we can't escape! God won't save us from our karma, we are answerable and accountable to our True Self, which is watching us every moment, in the highest court of this universe!

Religion provides a window of hope—both reasonable and unreasonable—for those who struggle to make both ends meet. Interestingly, it is seen as an insurance policy by those who have enough to eat and consume, but fear losing it and, therefore, want more to remain secure. Sadly, it is also used to exploit the intrinsic human fear against uncertainty in life and death by leaders and merchants of religions. Unfortunately, it is also used as a tool by politicians who wish to rule others.

> *Peace and quiet are not weaknesses; they are virtues, which reflect our culture, education and upbringing, and civility. We are a product of both nature and nurture.*

You Are Restless till Your Locus is Outside

Anything you don't receive at home, you seek outside, mostly with strangers. That includes *Attention, Appreciation and Acknowledgement*—the 3 'A's.

Your phone and social media have become your lifelines. You can't simply live without them; they provide you with cheap oxygen. You sleep with your phone. Your eyes and fingers crave to feel it otherwise they feel suffocated. Your eyes breathe through your phone. Machines exploits your hedonic needs and lure you more and more into virtual and material worlds, which lack the air of happiness. That is why you remain constantly restless and in search of real love and attention.

If you cannot notice me—what I eat, where I go or what I wear—what is the purpose of my being? Zilch! How do I justify my existence? What is the use of eating expensive food at a fancy restaurant, or wearing expensive clothes or going for expensive holidays, if people don't notice what you are doing? It is all a show; you are controlled by others and what others think about you. It is all about making a point to others that you are much wealthier and more successful than them. Otherwise, what is the point of your becoming wealthy and successful if others don't notice and become jealous of you? You just wanted to be noticed and appreciated.

Externalising the source of one's (hedonic) happiness is a recipe for misery. The hedonic happiness—achieved through those five senses of ours—depletes much faster than you can even realise. No surprise you are constantly in want of more, and more. Our needs have become hedonic as the disease of materialism has gripped us. National economies run based on exploitation of our materialistic greed. Multinationals have dedicated teams to keep a close watch on our every step and every facial gesture, through our use of mobile phone and the internet, and those numerous hidden video cameras in public places. We are being constantly watched through a clandestine international operation for data gathering. Do you know data management is the new professional career option?

Internalising one's happiness and following a path of altruism brings in plenty of longer-lasting joy and deeper satisfaction and, in fact, truly serves the purpose of one's existence on this planet. Otherwise, what is the difference between that stray dog and me; both exist, consume, scavenge and breed? If only we followed a more spiritual path, we would not be so miserable and such attention seekers, like toddlers. Of course, for that, one has to be gifted naturally with a deeper spiritual disposition. But is it also a matter of choice? Perhaps, yes.

Judgement

What if God spoke to you and said: I am the infinite and not like you humans. I can't reward you or punish you. Your own intentions and actions (and inactions) will judge you. Stop praying to me for material favours and forgiveness. I can't pardon you or reward you for your trespasses against your fellow beings. All beings are dear to me, all beings come from me and I am in all beings. I can't reward you for taking my name in vain or killing other beings in my name. If you love me, love all beings that you see around you. They will eventually judge you and reward or punish you, as is the case.

He kept wondering for a long time why his father was becoming increasingly paranoid about the intake of fruits and dairy products. One day, he suddenly realised he must actually be grateful to his father for his dietary preferences. His father was potentially saving him hefty medical expenses normally incurred by older people, mainly due to infections and weaker bones.

Doors and windows allow life to breathe and thrive. Without them, any structure, howsoever big and strong it may be, is completely useless and dead. Doors act as flexible, makeshift walls and provide the necessary security and privacy to the end-users of the house, whilst also allowing all important movement of life in and out of the house. Windows allow the air and sunlight to enter the house, which are important for the health and survival of the house dwellers.

Human body is like a structure. Its openings act as its doors and windows, which are necessary for its survival and growth. Philosophically, however, mind is the most important window of humans. Its openness and flexibility define a human being. A closed mind sows seeds of instability around it and can also unleash disaster in the wider world. When we don't regularly go on our internal journey, and sit and talk with our Self, and try to decipher the true nature and needs of our Self, and the direction that we should be heading into, life has its own ways of shaking and waking us up, and violently breaking our shackles and kicking us hard enough so that we are unknowingly pushed in our true direction to do what we are born to do.

Rise above religion, caste, region and gender if you want to make this world a better place for your children. Be prepared to be called a leftist by rightists and a rightist by leftists, as the world is polarised. Dodge them both by lifting yourself above them to a more global human level.

As our consciousness grows and expands, our human body struggles to catch up. Our spirit feels like breaking free to continue its expansion. That is why, with yog (meditation), physical yogic exercises are also recommended. Taichi and other outdoor aerobic exercises are also useful to restore equilibrium between the two entities—spirit and body.

God—He or She—is all pervading—within and without—in everyone and everything that we see and feel. We are inseparable from God. Air and water too can't be separated from us. Can air be seen? No, but its effects are seen! All we need to do is to go within and seek ourselves. The main branches of a large tree tend to grow in different directions, for creating their individual spaces to grow and to receive their own share of sunlight. As they grow, they appear to drift away from one another. But look carefully and you will see they are all connected to the same one trunk and nourished by the same roots. Religions are like those branches, connected to the same ONE eternal TRUTH. We humans are like those leaves on those branches. Let there be constructive competitions between the proponents of all religious faiths and philosophies about how good, noble, humanist and moralistic are our respective religions!

> *Each one of us is like a tree, nourished and challenged by the elements, but nurtured solely by our roots. Our (spiritual and overall) growth is determined by the depth and extent of our roots and their proximity to the groundwater, which is our Antaratma or the Super-consciousness. We are connected with one another through our roots.*

Such competitions will bring out the best in each one of us. Let people strive and compete for goodness, for being good, moral and just humans.

It is such joy being in the company of birds and animals, and observing their movements. They are so beautiful; they represent the purer form of natural energy. They live in the moment.

Jesus and Kashmir

It is believed there is a strong connection between Jesus and Kashmir. A reputable Kashmiri author, Prof Fida Hassnain, wrote several books on Jesus Christ, based on his lifelong, extensive, global research on the subject. His book, *Jesus in the East*, provides an invaluable, well researched, account about possible connection of Jesus with Kashmir and his life there. In the book, Jesus is believed to have been called Yuzu Asaf and his last resting place is believed to be Rozbal, in Srinagar, Kashmir. It is believed that Jesus spent the last years (14 years) in Kashmir, for which there is no account in the Bible. Note that, at that time, Kashmir was known worldwide as an important seat of learning.

It is also believed that, after his Resurrection, Jesus returned to Kashmir. St Thomas (known as 'Doubting Thomas') is believed to have touched him—to verify if his form was real—after his Resurrection. Prof Hassnain has made extensive references to Kalhana's *Rajatarangni,* as well as numerous Tibetan, Persian and other literature globally. The book marks an important part of our distant history.

After three decades of suffering and contemplation, I have discovered faith in my own Kashmiri blood, although lots of my blood has seeped into the sacred land of my Kashmir. I am confident our rishis, peers and fakirs will bless us if we all Kashmiris come close, join hands and work together. They are ready with their blessings.

From space one can see the earth, but not the individual people. Similarly, don't expect God to see you or listen to you individually unless, of course, God is omnipresent. Realise and remember the truth (of omnipresence) next time when you intend to rob anyone or wish anyone bad. You look for God everywhere but I see God in you.

Close your eyes, you will see me. I am in you and you are in me. And then the movie stops suddenly, the screen turns dark and the names roll by but not many pay attention to them. One must then carry oneself out of the hall and face the real life again.

Don't cry on my shoulder, as I may start crying too and my tears may drown both of us. My tears contain the tears of millions like me, but your tears are only yours. Support me as I must support you. Don't cry, stand and walk with me.

> *As we evolve spirituality, we begin to see ourselves in every living and non-living being. Our love for our child begins to resemble our love for all humans and flora and fauna. We transcend and outgrow our finite form.*

Flowers of a Garden

A person who claims 'there are differences in people' has not observed or thought enough. God has made no mistakes in designing humans; people are like flowers of God's garden. If we differentiate between people—based on religion, caste, creed, gender or ethnicity—we commit blasphemy and sin against God, which the Creator shall never forgive.

The more I travel, the more I discover the oneness of humans and existence of one global village. During my travels and social interactions, I have found that people everywhere in the world look same, with one pair of eyes, one pair of ears, one nose with two nostrils, one mouth with a tongue and teeth, one pair of arms and hands, and one pair of legs and feet. They all eat, walk and run, sleep, smile and laugh, and breed and answer the call of nature in a similar manner. Their animal instincts, thinking patterns and emotions, and social behaviours are also very similar. Then I wonder why do we humans fight? Is it only for the control, physical and economic, of power and authority?

In the last two years, I visited India 14 times and covered most of the country, except the east. I have found Indians are no different from Pakistanis or Bangladeshis or Persians or Australians or New Zealanders or the British or Americans or Canadians or Africans or Europeans or SE Asians or Asians. Except some local cultural differences, no other major differences exist between humans. With travel and globalisation, humans get exposed to other cultures and discover local variants of their own self and their own (ever-changing) culture, so their fear from other humans disappears and personal tolerance increases. Therefore, travel is important to breakdown the surficial human barriers and to bring humans closer; it also keeps the human mind healthy and positive, just like the flowing waters. Humans share 99.7% of the same DNA. Fruit flies, as a species, have more variation than humans.

Parts of the Same Body

Yes, they belong to a different faith than mine. But they are all humans, as I am. We were born from the same soil and we will return to the same soil. They belong to me as much as I belong to them. How can I rejoice when they are in pain? Their suffering is my suffering.

If your empathy is religion-specific, your humanness is dwarfed by your religious bias. You have not grown and truly become a human. Your religious faith was supposed to make you a disciplined, moral human being. It was never intended to make you a discriminatory, judgmental and prejudiced person against your fellow humans who follow other religious faiths. Being an empathetic, moral human is the only aim of humanism.

You were born to realise yourself and become a good human being—noble, moral, just and disciplined. Instead, why did you choose to be discriminatory? Could you not see that the other human being is just like you, your image? What made you blind? God lives in its own creation, God lives in every being. Respecting fellow humans is respecting God. Nothing happens without God's will. I must accept all people as they are. In essence, they are also my own versions.

I think I am capable enough to lead and accommodate everyone.

After all, we all belong to one human family. If I show intolerance, anyone else can show it too, which may not be acceptable to me. So, don't misuse the "unfriend" button and don't be intolerant.

The more I travel around our planet, the more I see my own reflection in other humans of different lands—from different cultures, creed, colours, languages etc. No cultural shocks for me in our lovely global village.

As I wrote thought, slept, watched a movie, and regularly ate my refreshments and refreshed, the plane flew smoothly, nonstop for 15 hours. The pilots and the cabin crew played their respective roles well. Later, at the carousel, I shook the hands that had flown my plane. The pilots smiled, thanked me in return and walked away tall and proud. I kept thanking them silently; they had done their job well. There is no need to call them by any other name.

We fall asleep or choose to sleep on a plane only because we have faith in our pilots and we trust our pilots will not sleep while flying. Such faith is implied the moment we buy the ticket. No expressed guarantees that we will be transported safely to our point of destination are provided by anyone. We take a leap of faith. Faith and trust keep the world going. We entrust our lives with the plane manufacturer, the maintenance staff and the pilots when we fly. Similar is the case with doctors, drug manufacturers and the chemists. The list goes on.

Your world lives inside you. You are the god of your internal world. Design your seasons. Let there be light! Bask in your sunshine. During night, turn your heart-light on and flood every nook and corner of your mind.

Gods can't be mortals. They have no need for a nose to breathe or a mouth to eat. They can't look like us humans. Perhaps, they do, who knows? Is that important? I must work (or beg) to put food on the table. How silly of me to take myself seriously. Gods must be smiling but only if they are able to see me.

Many of us are the most dangerous beings on the planet but some of us are also like God's own angels. There are many who live to kill other people and there are many who constantly strive to save lives. To maintain a stable equilibrium, let us find ourselves in the latter group.

At bedtime, none of us can be certain that he or she will wake up alive the next morning.

When children try to get away from parents, parents don't punish them. They wait till the children return. Love tolerates all trespasses. Love is patient. Love is God. God is love. Empathise and reach out to others who need a hand. Realise yourself in them. They are another form of yours. Life connects you with them through your spirit. Spirituality binds this world; religions create divisions. If you too use the terms 'they' and 'we', you feed the divisions.

No material in the world can buy the experience of freedom—- the absolute freedom, when you are your own master and you are your own slave. It can be a divine exhilarating feeling beyond any human imagination.

How often does a mother want to severely punish and possibly kill her baby for being a rebel, rowdy and mischievous? How can then leaders of a country punish those citizens who don't believe in them?

Nature made this world and we humans bred right from the time the first woman and the first man evolved on our unique planet. Since then, we humans have incessantly kept biologically producing more and more humans, albeit for various reasons. It is we humans who produce our children, God does not! We humans also created religions, at different times, for various reasons too, God did not.

If you argue everything is created by God, then accept all kinds of people around you and their religious thoughts. Don't hate and fight them off. If you do, you are fighting God. Blasphemy, isn't? You can't accept some and reject some, as per your personal choice and convenience. Either accept God's Will and stay quiet, or take the responsibility and be accountable for everything that happens around you. There are reasons why things have happened in the past and why they are happening now. Visit the reasons before blaming and stereotyping others. It is useful that one introspects deeply.

Let us all enrol in a school where we learn to introspect, contemplate and do everything possible to promote peace and humanity on this beautiful planet of ours. We have one earth, one sun, one moon and one God. So we are ONE. Let us talk peace. Nothing that you think you have belongs to you, not even your body. Your body neither obeys you nor acts as per your whims or wishes. It functions independent of you, even when you fall asleep. One day it will shut down whether you want it or not. Be humble and wise. Realise who you truly are when you still have the time and the opportunity.

When one part of the body is in pain, how can other parts of the body remain painless or rejoice? All parts of the body are connected through the nervous system. Similarly, all people in the world are connected through spirituality. Transcend the manmade divisions. Connect and empathise. Except your own self, no one is your enemy. Befriend yourself. Attain peace. Radiate peace. We are one large global family, inter-dependant. Let us look after one another, as we look after our individual nuclear families.

Who am I? Why am I here? Have I known it, that I may have to depart anytime? The Maker can switch off the supply of my breaths any moment.

Sleep is one of the best gifts that we receive from nature. For availing it though, we must completely surrender to it. After falling asleep, however, no one can be certain if one will wake up. Same is the case with the gift of love. Surrender is the precondition for receiving these gifts.

Look after your core and the foundation, go within yourself every day and know yourself. While you feed you five material senses, your soul suffers from starvation. It is a matter of time before you wilt and wither away.

It is the destiny of some fruit that they are squeezed, crushed, pulped and squashed for releasing their juice. Not many can understand the pain that they endure in the process. Imagine how hard we try to squeeze that last drop of lemon or orange juice out of its shell. Artists are like fruit.

Life squeezes out every drop of juice (art) that it can to share it with the wider world. It is pain that produces their juice and it is indeed pain only that extracts it from them. The more juice they produce and contain, the more pain they endure in releasing it. It is their destiny. Gold and diamonds endure unimaginable heat, cutting and grinding from both nature and their maker before they shine and glitter.

Many people claiming to be religious and spiritual are seen to indulge in most irreligious and immoral activities. Spirituality must flows in actions and not through one's mouth. Religion is meant to be lived, for spiritual elevation and make good human beings, and not to be used for grabbing power or harassing other people.

A Persian poet wrote: "I waited and waited, and suffered in waiting, for the flower to blossom. And then the wind blew it away suddenly." Is the poet implying his suffering is permanent although the flower was transitory?

Pain and troubles must liberate our soul. One can't keep feeding the divisions which give us the pain and suffering in the first place. God did not make the divisions, we humans did. Nature does not differentiate. Blood groups don't differentiate, neither do diseases. Empathy conquers all. Love overarches everything.

This and That—We Seek

We seek what we don't have; we seek what we have lost;
We seek the unknown; we seek our self.
We seek love; we seek attention;
We seek power; we seek the authority.
We seek knowledge; we seek the truth;
Not a moment passes when we don't seek.
We seek with our eyes open; we seek with our eyes closed;
We seek when we are awake; we seek when we are asleep.
Wandering minds; that is what we are;
We seek this and that till we breathe our last.

It is lonely at the top

Wise and intelligent people waste their time in discussing powerful people

FOUR

RELATIONSHIPS IN LIFE

Commitment

Commitment is born out of love and care for others, as well as out of duty and responsibility towards your country and/or the world community. In this materialistic day and age, commitment may be seen by some as madness. But it is the only way one can live and demonstrate one's love and care for others. Talking love is one thing, but walking it is another thing. Care is another version of love. This world runs because of committed, relatively mad people, and not selfish commentators and witnesses. Only those people who work and live for others really live; some are acknowledged and remembered for doing their bit and making a positive difference in this world, whereas others just exist.

People who live and move in air-conditioned environment, wine and dine with the rich and the famous, and manipulate others for their personal gains, will never understand the concept of commitment to others, as it clashes with their selfish tendencies. Nature levels off everything in the end when karma catches up!

Soldiers, who man the country's borders in extreme discomfort and risk their lives, as well as farmers, who toil hard on the ground and in extreme weather conditions to grow our food, demonstrate extremely high levels of commitments towards humanity and their country. Some people may (carelessly) brush it off, saying that they do it just for earning their daily bread. Well that is a fact, because they and their families too need to thrive, but that does not explain everything and why they do what they do. The truth is much beyond their personal survival.

On a much smaller scale though, commitment is taking your pet for his morning walk when it is drizzling at the time you start from home, and then getting drenched to the bone halfway through the walk due to a heavy downpour that no umbrella can withstand, with weather forecast indicating rain through the entire day. Huskies need regular walks—preferably twice daily. Sakha, our husky, was in a kennel for the last one week, as his parents were overseas on work. On his return home, he needed a quick walk at the earliest, so no excuses could/would/should work. Some people may term such commitment as sheer foolishness and scoff at the entire act. But that is what is called commitment.

Friendship

Friendship used to be a matter of intellectual and emotional compatibility, chemistry in simple words—and sharing common interests; a subjective matter, generally. It would happen naturally. No longer! Over time, the definition of friendship has more or less changed; it has become more and more objective and strategic. These days, the best of friends turn into the worst of foes, if their individual interests cross paths. On the other side, sworn enemies forge strategic alliances for common interests. This happens in families and communities too. It is not easy to separate friends from enemies. One never knows who is carrying a hidden dagger to stab you in your back especially at a time when you would be most unsuspecting. Anyone can surprise you most unexpectedly, either way. Faces are deceptive, so are smiles, handshakes and hugs.

Man is after all a herd animal, but with a difference. Unlike most other animals, man is very conniving, scheming and deceptive.

If anyone trusts you blindly and unconditionally, you are extremely fortunate, a god's angel. Never ever break that trust even if you have to lose your life. In return, trust that person blindly. Such mutual trust is divine, it has god's blessings.

> *Now, people think before making friends; it used to be a matter of heart in the past.*

A True Friend

A true friend lends a genuine ear when one needs to vent one's heart and mind. Patient listening—without judging, gagging or interrupting—is the most important friendly gesture one can show. A true friend never provides unsolicited or condescending advice or hurtful comments unless one is running a risk of falling or may have fallen prey to material or moral corruption, violence, alcohol, drug addiction, gambling etc. A true friend provides honest advice, without political correctness, howsoever bitter that may be, but only when any such advice is solicited.

> *A true friend provides all possible help—without delay, excuses, hesitation or interrogation—when requested. Compassion, care and empathy are the foundation of true friendship.*

Listen, Listen, Listen

Active listening is the mantra for fair and caring parents, effective teachers, efficient managers, successful employers and benevolent governments and all those individuals and organizations who wield disproportionate power over their stakeholders.

Where parents don't listen to their children, they effectively lose them. As soon as they grow up, children become rebellious. Similarly, where managers don't pay attention to their staff, the efficiency of their organisation becomes low and the staff turnover becomes high. Similarly, where a government doesn't listen to the public, it loses respect, faith and trust of people, leading to discontent amongst the stakeholders and potential uprising in some cases where their democratic rights are seen to get compromised. History is full of numerous examples of such authoritarian, repressive and dictatorial regimes that caused significant damage to the country they ruled.

Every human strives for freedom of expression, thought and action, provided their freedom does not trespass or infringe the freedom of their fellow beings. Humans—poor or rich, uneducated or educated, employees or employers—are born with intrinsic expectation to be respected, including by their parents and loved ones.

Active listening reflects the respect that you show to a person. Listen or rue the consequences.

Human Relationships

Human relationships are as complex as humans. Relationships fail because one partner takes their relationship for granted. Relationships must be nurtured, regardless of love, for them to survive. In a loving relationship, if two lovers start taking each for granted and don't commit to nurturing their relationship on a daily basis, one or both of them are likely to start looking elsewhere. Humans look elsewhere for what they don't get at home. Pure human psychology!

We love flowers, but if we don't water them, they wilt fast. Love alone is no guarantee that they will survive. Similarly, a relationship needs to be nurtured in the same manner. Where two people love each other, they must never take each for granted; otherwise they will potentially lose each other. Where individuals constantly fear they may potentially lose the other person if the other person feels he or she is being taken for granted, people remain cautious. They nourish their relationship religiously and don't take things for granted.

Pride and self-respect, and sometimes ego, invariably gets the better of most of us. No person likes to be taken for a ride or for granted in any relationship, whether it is a parental relationship or a relationship between siblings. The risks increase significantly in friendships and romantic or matrimonial relationships.

In this day and age, a typical family does not live as one unit, with a shared common vision, interest and values. Instead, a family comprises individuals living in one house, with varied individual interests and wants. Each member seeks outside the home what it lacks in the home. At home, when it is supposed to be family time in a traditional sense, each one of them invariably remains engaged with other people, on chatting platforms and social media, using their phones.

If you don't want to lose the other person, don't play around. Make the other person feel wanted, loved and needed every single day, just as the earth spins and presents us sunrise every day, or the way you brush your teeth every day. Show your commitment to the relationship. Work proactively towards maintaining it in good health for ensuring its longevity. Never ever even think of taking your relationship for granted if you can't afford to see it dying.

Sincere human relationships differ from casual kicks and thrills in essence and character. Casual thrills bring nothing but tears. If your so-called friends 'show' respect or love to you based on your 'perceived' wealth, position, authority and influence; or your good looks, expensive clothes, cars, house or the locality that you live in, they are all fake. They just want to use you so that they can use the things that you possess. They shall undoubtedly have no interest in you if you lose the things that you possess now. Help yourself and find your real friends. Be one to have one. You will be extremely lucky if you are able to find only five real friends if not more.

Relationships—personal, social or business—thrive on a win-win basis, where shared values and interests are nurtured by both parties. Where one party attempts to maximise the output whilst minimising its input, the equilibrium shifts fast towards instability and collapse. Longevity of any relationship depends essentially on the selflessness and mutual respect between the parties. Mutual distrust and selfishness of one or both parties undermines it fast. Spontaneity, or the absence of it, differentiates an authentic relationship from a formal one. In formal relationships, people tend to think about the political aspect of the relationship, which causes a time lag and murders the innocent spontaneity.

Complications—in matters of politics or relationships, are usually deliberate, to camouflage the truth. It is generally caused by conniving, selfish and mischievous people. Stupid people also tend to complicate simple matters. One who makes tall claims about complexity in a seemingly simple matter, or condescendingly tells you that you cannot understand it, most probably has not understood the problem himself. If you cannot explain a certain problem, from any imaginable aspect of life, to your uneducated grandparents, you have not possibly understood it yourself.

We tend to blame others for our failures and miseries, as most of us choose to suffer from memory loss. Those of us who can analyse the cause and effect of their past actions, inactions and misadventures will find no one else but themselves to blame. What goes around comes around. *We reap what we sow.*

Elder siblings must not compete with their younger siblings or try to alienate or compromise them. They have the responsibility to look after their younger siblings and the family. In the past, after parents, the eldest sibling would be seen as the model figure by his/her younger siblings. He/she would also care and look after them just as parents would. Many would leave their studies and work to earn money for the family if the father died. This analogy applies to countries too. The original inhabitants of a nation are those eldest siblings.

Love is the most misunderstood and misinterpreted term. In any shape or form, however, it is not an entitlement or a matter of right. It can't be measured. In most practical and tangible form, it is reflected in care and empathy. If one exhausts one's time from one's invaluable life-bank and resources from one's sweat and blood in caring for you, that is love in its most pure form. Our parents are the best examples of love. In some cases, our teachers too exemplify it. In most other relationships, love and care are subject to one's mood, need, pride and ego.

Feelings are usually mutual. By natural law, our thoughts for any person are mirrored towards us by that person. If you wish to be perceived with love by any person, you must harbour similar thoughts for that person. Love begets love. Your hate too will be reciprocated.

She suspected her husband of infidelity. He protested repeatedly and provided many clarifications, but all in vain. Not believing him, she decided to punish him by doing exactly what she imagined him to be doing. Suspicion and revenge made her much worse than she had suspected her husband to be. She ended up being a public wife.

Love them but don't let them start hating you. They don't know what real love is; they are not used to it. They may feel threatened and doubt you. They can't just imagine one could really love unconditionally. If you love truly, surrender fully.

You don't need social network for partying alone during your sunny days; you need it much more for your rainy days. Your true friends are only those who will support you and stand by you in your most difficult times. You are fortunate if you have three such true friends.

Love means losing yourself—unconditionally. Love has no room for ego. Don't kill your love; push your ego out when dealing with people you love and don't want to lose.

In our quest to connect with the world, we became disconnected with ourselves. Our greatest enemies become the tools and gadgets closest to us—our smart phones and laptops. Our freedom from the web we weaved around us lay in surgical separation of these fetters from us, but we failed, and we failed miserably. We got addicted to technology, abusing and misusing it. We created our own monster that devoured us, slowly, bit by bit and we ended up being zombies, humanoids and robots, sans feelings and emotions.

> *We connected nonstop with the world out there but remained disconnected with ourselves. We reached out to the stars but uprooted ourselves. We satisfied our senses but starved our soul. We befriended others but not ourselves. We existed more but lived less.*

Endeavour to 'give' rather than to 'take' is an essential condition for maximising the health and positive dynamics of any relationship.

True Love—Just Behold Me, Don't Touch Me

I stood proud, beautiful and pristine. I loved my free spirit. One day, your rowdy younger brother tried to outrage my modesty and I requested you to protect me. Reluctantly you did protect me on the condition that I live with you. I agreed to stay with you on the condition you allow a screen to stand between us, which allowed you to see and enjoy my beauty, but you were not meant to touch me. Practically, it meant nothing as I was too weak and you could always touch me at will but it was a symbolic reminder of the promise you made to me.

Over time, you made several holes in the screen and would push your arms through them and touch me, and I would protest. When your rowdy younger brother would try to intrude under the guise of trying to free me from you, I was lashed and I would bleed at times.

Finally, one day, in broad daylight, without informing me and seeking my consent, you threw away the old damaged screen between us and I lay before you, naked and stunned. You gagged me so that people don't hear my wailing cries. You lie to the world everything is well with me but don't allow anyone to see my condition and hear me. You declared openly to the world that you have the right to touch me at will as I belonged to you. You broke your promise. You intend to outrage my modesty. I see lust in your eyes and your mouth is watering in anticipation of your consumption of me. You craved to consume me. You tell the world the screen had left me poor all these years, as your prosperity did not reach me due to the screen. But the truth is, even now, I am much wealthier than you.

Who does not know you are so poor? The truth is you can't give me something that you don't have. You are merely lying just for your lust. Deceitfully, you intend to turn me into your prostitute and steal my wealth. I shall never give in to your greed and lust. I shall fight.

I prefer death to prostitution. I am still proud and free spirited. Just behold me, don't touch me. Don't let your corrupted love desecrate my sacred space.

Many historical places of worship in Kashmir—eg at Anantnag and Khrew—are characterised by large sacred ponds, lined with cobbled-stone pitching and fed by natural springs. Sulphur-rich spring waters attracted people with skin diseases. People enjoyed holy dips in those ponds but did not desecrate them. Many ponds teemed with fish—called 'naag-gaad' (spring fish)—but catching or consuming such fish was forbidden. There were stories about people who had dared and consumed such naag-gaad and then faced unfortunate consequences from nature.

We rely on most others for our survival, sustenance, security and prosperities. Surprisingly, we don't fully accept others as they are; we draw a line—'them' and 'us'. We claim superiority to 'them'. In our global village of mutual reliance and common human issues and challenges, we talk about nationalism. We are regressive.

Empathy, compassion and selfless care for others define the level of growth in a human being. Alarmingly, as a result of human degradation, these virtues are also seen as signs of 'weakness' and 'cowardice' in complex socio-political situations when felt and publicly shown towards 'them' in the current polarised world of 'them' and 'us'. It always does matter what kind of an action we do—good or bad, selfish or selfless, noble or evil, mundane or spiritual, physical or mental, laboured or intellectual—but what matters more is how we do that action. Any action that has the potential to seriously affect millions of other lives must be undertaken with extreme care and caution, with due consideration of human sensitivities, and only after patiently undertaking a sincere consultative process.

> *A path that traverses through selfless inclusivism, forgiveness and sincerity will alone lead us to a sustainable and peaceful future. Respect towards our neighbours, cohabitants and even adversaries, and sincere engagement with them to share our human and natural resources are the need of the hour to keep the human race alive.*

Materialism imprisons

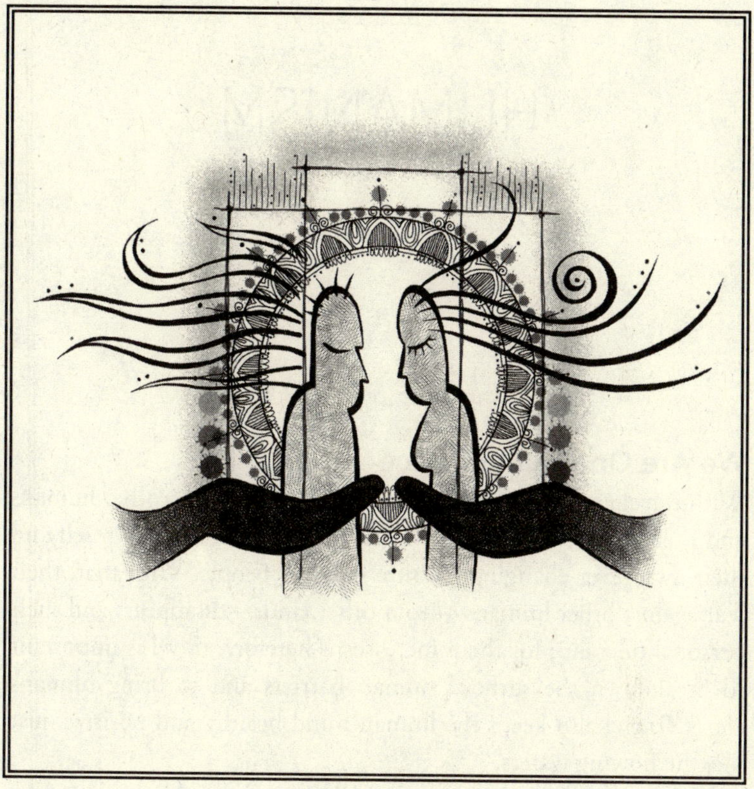

Gender equality

FIVE

HUMANISM

We Are One Human Race

With travel and globalisation, humans get exposed to other humans and their cultures. They discover local variants of their own self and their own (ever-changing) culture in other people. With that, their fear against other humans—from other lands—disappears and their personal tolerance for them increases. Therefore, travel is important to breakdown the surficial human barriers and to bring humans closer. Travel also keeps the human mind healthy and positive, just like the flowing waters.

The more I travel, the more I discover the oneness of humans and existence of one global village. During my travels and social interactions, I have found that people everywhere in the world have similar physical features. Everywhere on the earth, humans are born with one pair of eyes, one pair of ears, one nose with two nostrils, one mouth with a tongue and teeth, one pair of arms and hands, and one pair of legs and feet. They all eat, walk and run, sleep, smile and laugh, and breed and answer the call of nature in a similar manner.

Their animal instincts, thinking patterns and emotions, and social behaviours are also very similar.

I wonder why then do we humans fight against one another? Why do we humans differentiate other humans from one another? Is it only for gaining control—physical and economic—over them or is it an intrinsic human tendency to achieve and enjoy power and authority over other livings beings, including other humans?

We may have moved from the pre-Industrial Age to the current, post-Industrial Age of globalisation but, deep inside, we are still living in the distant past to a large extent. Despite globalisation, we remain aware of the (surficial) differences between 'others' and 'us'. These differences generally give rise to mutual apprehensions, fear and hate, sometimes violence. Humans have a fair way to go.

> *Unless we shake off the mentality of the past, dump the past baggage and embrace the oneness of human race, we will continue to ruin our present with violence. There will be not much peace in the world. The human race needs to take a global leap of faith to jump from the past to the present. Let us embrace humanism.*

Humans

Human methods of survival are uniquely their own, many methods are conniving in nature. Most humans are natural actors, multi-faced, rubber-faced and many with occasion-based masks. Some don't even remember their own real face. They put on an innocent face, without ego or pride, when they need help. But once their needs are met, their ego returns and they put on an entirely different face, with pride and sometimes with fangs. Many also bite the hands that may have fed them in the past. For their individual survival, many don't hesitate in compromising others.

Do good and forget if you belong to a minority of soft-hearted, benevolent, helpful individuals. But that is easier said than done. Good humans are humans only, mortals and complete with expectations, and not gods. Even gods are believed to have expectations. Aren't gods believed to punish if they are not worshipped and given offerings? Don't you prostrate before them when begging them for kindness and favours? The world runs on expectations. Hypocrites are those who claim to live and help without expectations. Either they don't help others or they just lie. Be prepared to be stung back when you help. You will be lucky if you aren't.

> *Humans are enigmatic to an extent but, as with machines, human mysteries and secrets can also be deciphered. It takes a human with an expert eye to decode another human. During WWII, British had reportedly decoded even the seemingly unbreakable German code machine, Enigma.*

Human Animals

In the distant past, morality, ethics and justice used to be considered as virtues, but now these words figure only in text books and school lessons. Practically, it is 'might, deceit and trickery' that is the order of the day. People learn these traits from home and powerful people. Politicians use these weapons unashamedly. If misleading, cooked and blatant lies, and half-truths can get the job done, why not?

Evidently, in terms of ethics, animals are much higher than humans. Animals are not greedy and conniving as we are, they kill and eat only when they are hungry. The human greed has no limit. We humans are the most dangerous animals on the planet. We have made all kinds of weapons of mass destruction. We have ruined the environment. We have gobbled up the natural resources. We kill our own kind.

Expecting others to be good, as a condition, before us taking the necessary initiatives to be good, does not help our human race.

Mass Killers

Thinking about it, how ironical is it that mass killers, who claim to fight for any mission (howsoever, noble or just that mission may be) cause and contribute to immense suffering and irreparable damage to the mission and the image of their own community whom they claim to represent.

The killers also selfishly ignore the fact that there will be serious repercussions of their violent act, which their community members will have to face. Violence is never accepted or forgotten by people. As a psychological reaction, people tend to forever stereotype the members of the killer's community, howsoever peaceful and humane they may otherwise be. In most cases, they also face ramifications for no individual fault of theirs.

This sad irony of life goes on to prove that terrorists are not friends of anyone, neither their own community nor the people they target.

> *Let us rise, transcend the man-made divisions and be humans, and try to make this world a better place for our children.*

Silent Philanthropy is What Makes Us Human

My mother was a noble person—a devoted mother and a natural philanthropist in her own right. Out of her meagre savings from everyday household expenses, she would quietly help many close relatives and neighbours—through both cash and kind. Once she reattached and healed the severed right-hand thumb of a Kashmiri mason who had constructed our house in Kashmir. Following her demise at a young age, many people flew from Kashmir to offer condolences. Her teachings include:

- Never wish bad for anyone, not even your worst enemies, as it may come back and haunt you one day. You never know the whole story—the bigger picture. You don't know what wrongs you may have done in your past lives.
- If you can't do good to anyone, don't try to do any bad too.
- If your right hand is helping anyone, your left hand must not know about it.

My grandfather was a hidden philanthropist. He was a reputed teacher; he taught Mathematics and English at high school level. Outside school, he also privately tutored thousands of students—

Muslims and Pandits—in Kashmir, Jammu and Ladakh, many of them absolutely free of cost. In addition, he also quietly sponsored the education of many students from lower socio-economic strata. His funeral was attended by thousands of people.

Unselfish empathy, compassion and care, without bias or discrimination, defines humanity in its best form. Expecting others to be good, as a condition, before us taking the necessary initiatives to be good, does not help our human race.

We Link Our Elders With Our Youngsters

Who is responsible for the care and nurture of our elders—the government or the society or the children? Are elders purely at the whim and mercy of their children? Where are the traditional values? What has happened to the traditional family structure? Why are nuclear families becoming selfish?

In this day and age, due to a fast erosion of traditional human and family values, caused mainly due to materialism and a growing competition, many unfortunate elderly parents are neglected and abused by their children. In many cases, they are completely abandoned by their children. In the past, a closely knitted social fabric, with proactive involvement of neighbours and relatives, would become a major deterrent against any such occurrence. Due to political correctness these days, neighbours are less likely to get involved.

Our elders are our most valuable brain trust and we must humbly listen to them and consider their invaluable advice on matters of life. Likewise, we must also listen to our youngsters and be sensitive to their behaviour patterns; they reflect how life is evolving, as of now. By observing and listening to our youngsters, we should be able to visualise and caution them against potential pitfalls and challenges lying in the paths that they may be treading, and suggest better alternatives. And, where we fall short, we must refer to our most valuable brain trust, our elders, who have lived and understood life much more than us. We are the link. Let us stay strong and act wisely to help shape a better future of this world.

We are the all-important link between our elders and our younger generations. We act as adapters or conduits between them. The onus is always on us to connect our future generations with our roots, our elders.

It is better to be a good human before becoming anything else.

Our Parents Are Our Gods

Like all other mammals, we humans are also born from our parents. Our parents strive to protect us. They nourish us right from the time we are conceived in our mother's womb. After our birth, they strive very hard, day and night, to protect, nourish and nurture us till we become adults, and sometimes beyond our adulthood. Undoubtedly, therefore, they represent God. No one has even been, or will be, born or raised by Gods or deities, as imagined or believed in a traditional sense, without the parental involvement, support and endeavour.

Parents work tirelessly and sacrifice their personal comfort in supporting and growing their children till they attain adulthood and get educated. Unfortunately, many parents take hefty loans for the education and wedding of their children, which exacerbates and prolongs their financial instability, whilst adding to their physical/mental distress. They do it as their duty, so they think, and unconditionally, mainly due to the love and care for their children. After the completion of their education, most grownup children find jobs and gradually become financially independent. They marry and have children of their own. In the meantime, their parents also grow older. A time comes when parents retire from work. As a natural process, all humans become physically weaker after attaining a certain age, and parents are no exception. When children are young, they constantly need physical, emotional and financial support, which is unconditionally provided by their parents. A time comes when the roles—of care and nurture—are reversed and when parents too need to be looked after by their grown-up children. In many cases, unfortunately, grown-up children withdraw support from their parents and send them to old-age homes.

There is no bigger sin than abandoning one's parents at a time when they need their children the most. Shame on such individuals who abuse or abandon their parents in their old age!

Do We Need Social Policing?

Why are many unfortunate parents being abandoned by their grown-up children? It is important to understand the psychology underlying this social sickness. In many cases, the finger may point towards the parents themselves. Perhaps they failed to set personal good examples for their children. Perhaps they did not show enough love and care towards their own parents. What goes around comes around. Perhaps they encouraged their children to be too competitive and selfish. Perhaps they never inculcated good social and ethical values in their children. In a nutshell, it is extremely unfortunate to see many old parents abandoned by their well-off children, seemingly a direct result of degradation in the social and ethical values within the community.

In a developing country, such as India, where a robust social security system run by government is missing, a dedicated social policing force may perhaps be the need of the hour, the members of which are chosen by the local communities. To function effectively and serve its core objectives, such a force will require regular voluntary financial contributions and proactive ground support by the members of the community.

The social police, whilst keeping an eye on the families and individuals within the community and monitoring their social behaviour, must also endeavour to inculcate social and ethical values, as well as promote social responsibility within the community. In a country like India, it can also endeavour to bring about a number of urgent social reforms in the community, such as:

- Enforcement of simple wedding functions (costing not more than Rupees 1 lakh at the most);
- Prevention of occurrence of divorces;
- Penalisation of individuals who abandon their parents—through legal avenue, followed by social boycott;

- Use and promotion of the traditional language at homes; and
- Promotion and maintenance of spiritual, cultural and religious traditions.

How Can Parents Look After Themselves?

In this materialistic day and age, given a high probability of abandonment by their grown-up children, parents, especially In India, are strongly urged and encouraged that after they have discharged their parental duty till their children reach the age of 21, they must also earnestly work to safeguard their own personal interests and secure their own old age, by saving as much as possible and spending the least possible on their grown-up children.

Children should be made to wait to inherit the wealth of their parents—of course, at parents' sweet will and discretion—and only after the natural death of their parents. Similar to western countries, all youth must be encouraged and expected to work and meet their personal expenses after passing Year 12. In India's case, one may extend the parental support to the completion of the child's first degree (Bachelors). Thereafter, it must be an individual's responsibility to fund his/her personal costs and expenses related to his/her post-graduate degree, wedding and the house. Parents, of course, may make token contributions, but out of their own sweet will—like in western countries.

It may be strongly emphasised that parents must eventually be the responsibility of their children, and vice versa, and not the government or any other social organisation. No person should be allowed to get away with a sin of abandoning one's parents (or children), whatever be the reason. Old-age homes are meant only for those elders who have no children or any family to support them. In no case, old-age homes should be expected to house those elders who have healthy and able-bodied, grown-up and financially stable children, unless, out of their own will and volition, they opt to stay there for their own personal comfort.

A Warning for Grown-up Children

As per the *Law of Karma*, your children will do to you exactly what you do to your parents. Time flies fast and it will not be long before you see yourself in the shoes of your parents. It does not matter how much cash you have or how many bungalows you own or how many cars you drive; you are nothing if you don't have a family to go to. Your family is the only real wealth you are blessed with and your family includes your parents. Without your parents you are zilch—nothing! Cherish them till they are with you.

> *Let sanity prevail on us and we look after our parents and elders, as they look after their children and younger generations, otherwise our traditional family and community structures will be things of the past. And that may be the beginning of the end of the human race.*

Women Empowerment

Full empowerment of women, in all walks of life, is the key to world peace and progress. Only when a community dignifies its women and gives them full respect, honour and all privileges, it can be deemed as evolved and progressive.

Women must have equal representation in all affairs of the world, at all levels. They must empower themselves. Sensible men must proactively help to restore the social, ethical and moral equilibrium.

Instability in the social equilibrium and traditional religious bias against women could be deemed as a major cause underlying social violence, rape and global terrorism. Full empowerment and hundred percent education of women globally could possibly prove as a panacea in restoring sense, stability and peace in the world.

Woman, you represent the best part of the humankind. Nature has made you much more tenacious, resilient and tough than your male counterparts. You have already proven that you are equal and, in many cases, even much better than men in many aspects of life and living, at home and at the workplace. You represent Mother Nature, nurture and love. There is nothing that you can't do that men can do; you can do even better. You are far above in status than your male competitors. You are Saraswati, Kaali, Chandi and Laxmi. Just be yourselves. You are complete in yourselves. Believe in yourselves. Empower yourselves. You have to prove nothing to anyone. Thank you for keeping this world going and worth living in.

The sky has suddenly changed. God has turned around the social equation. Overnight, magically, India has become a matriarchal community. Dowry will now be paid by men, and not by women. Men will have to leave their parental homes and go and stay with the women's parents, where they will do all household chores, like women would do previously. Men will also carry and deliver babies, instead of women, and stay home to raise and look after their children.

Unless and until the women in India are not empowered to have full and genuine gender equality, with 100 percent education and employment, India will continue to fall far behind China.

> *Full empowerment of women—in all areas of life—is the key to world peace and progress. Only when a community dignifies its women and gives them full respect and all privileges can it be deemed as evolved and progressive.*
>
> *Woman, you represent the best part of the humankind. You have to prove nothing to anyone. You have already proven you are equal to, and actually better than, men in all aspects of life and living, at home and at the workplace.*

Unity in Diversity

Mutual respect, acceptance and tolerance between people coming from diverse ethnicities and religions is paramount, as building foundation blocks of freedom, for sustainable peace, health, happiness and progress of a sovereign country. Sovereignty and freedom come with responsibility, not only towards ourselves but towards all our fellow citizens.

The 26th day of January is celebrated as *Australia Day* in Australia and as *Republic Day* in India.

Kashmir (India) gave me birth, values and education. On Republic Day, the Constitution of India came into effect. India, one of the oldest civilisations on the planet, is the world's largest democracy, a fast growing economy and the world's second most populous country.

Australia gave me freedom, honour and dignity after adopting me as one of her own more than two decades ago. In this day and age, Australia Day marks the celebration of its social diversity and a diverse landscape. Originally, it marked the anniversary of the arrival of the First Fleet of British ships at Port Jackson, New South Wales, in 1788. Australia, the largest island country in the world, ranks high on liveability, happiness and prosperity. Being home to people coming from nearly 160 countries, Australia can be considered as a mini-world. To celebrate their unity in diversity, Australians proudly say, *"We are many, but we are one."* Australian politics and elections are not driven by race, religion or regional politics. Typically, environment and sustainability, national economy, people's health and socio-economic issues drive the current Australian politics.

We Lose Our Freedom if it is Misused or Abused

True lovers of freedom uphold the intrinsic human dignity and the freedom of all fellow humans. People must be allowed to exercise their rights and privileges responsibly and not allow divisive and polarising forces, internal or external, to harm their country and the world.

A country remains in the hands of people, who must look after it. People must vote with prudence and vision. Let us celebrate the human race and our humanness. We must commit ourselves to show acceptance and care for all fellow citizens, from all ethnic and religious backgrounds.

"United we stand, divided we fall", as a wise saying goes. We must learn from history and remain united to stay sovereign, otherwise history may repeat itself. Only when people remain united, their country remains integrated, strong, progressive, healthy and happy.

People, keep a close vigil and maintain communal harmony. Don't react to the provocation of terrorists who want to manipulate you. Don't fall for their inhuman, blasphemous, evil designs. Don't let them win. Terrorism, including terrorism in the name of God or religion, is the highest order of blasphemy against God. No cause, whatsoever, justifies killing other innocent beings. Humans can't carry out terrorist acts, so terrorists must be sub-humans. A bird-catcher lost all his birds, and even the net, when the netted birds flew off together in unison.

A community where inherent dignity of humans is not upheld, and where people are generally selfish and mainly worship wealth and power, is bound to be corrupt. Such a community will certainly decay and implode over time.

Endeavour to underpin the foundations of your country; don't undermine it by your rhetoric and extreme views on religion, politics and nationalism. Be a soldier of peace, not of hate, death and destruction. Human unhappiness due to terrorism in all its shades and forms—domestic, social, religious and political—will possibly continue unabated till the current power differentials between women and men, and between the poor and the rich, are not eradicated everywhere on our planet. It will also keep increasing as the world population increases.

If not by dialogue, should all disputes be settled by the gun? Does the gun also provide a solution to resolve inter and intra-family disputes and conflicts between neighbours? Since when have we become a trigger-happy community? Or, have we always been one? Thankfully, mad dreamers do exist in this world; otherwise there would be no electricity and light bulbs, planes and spacecrafts, mobile phones and the internet, underwater tunnels and sky bridges, and delicate organ transplants and cures for diseases.

If a community is deeply divided (along the lines of caste, region, religion, socio-economic), it is a no brainer that others can potentially, and surely will, exploit and deepen all such divisions for their gains. So why not erase the divisions? Why not glue and bind the people together? But it takes visionary people to do so. Erasing those divisions won't help the politicians in winning the elections, so no one will ever think of doing it.

If we lose our humanity, empathy, compassion and prudence, we will be no different than terrorists.

Being jingoistic is not being patriotic. Crying war on social media does not bring peace and prosperity.

If you are a patriot and truly committed to serve your country, then work to cement the existing social cracks. Help to build strong bridges between communities so that people can cohere peacefully. If we lose our humanity, empathy, compassion and prudence, we will be no different than terrorists.

Nothing Can Justify Murders by Cow Vigilantes

In the recent years, India has seen a spurt in lynching by cow-vigilantes. No law or religious belief whatsoever, in the world can justify such a growing menace of murdering humans—mostly belonging to the minority Muslim population—by cow-vigilantes, who mostly belong to the majority Hindu population, just on the basis of their apprehension or suspicion that the victim is going to kill a cow and eat or sell its meat. Ironically, the meat consumption has increased in India over the years. India also exports beef to other countries. All lives—humans and other animals—are precious.

Gender Equality

One extreme gives way to the other extreme. Anger begets anger. To every action, there is an equal and opposite reaction. Tit for tat! What goes around comes around. Do unto others what you wish them to do unto you. These are some of the phrases that fit into the context of this discussion on gender equality, feminism, misogyny and humanism.

If equality between the two genders is not proactively restored now, we'll see the rise of another extreme, where males will be at the receiving end. And then the cycle will continue—from one extreme to the other, like a continuously swinging pendulum.

The social and family life will continue to break down due to mutual distrust, fear and hatred. Let us visit history, not only of the past 100 years, but much older than that, of thousands of years, and then try to realise how women around the world were openly discriminated against through generations, not only by the religious and social systems but, sadly, also by their own families. Mischievously, as a male conspiracy, religion was used as a tool to do so—to control and exploit women. We must not repeat the misdeeds of our ancestors who were generally discriminatory against the women folk.

Our mothers and grandmothers have suffered, and their mothers and grandmothers have also suffered. They all lived second class lives in an unfair male-dominated patriarchal world. Ironically, most mothers in this day and age too show preference for male children and a clear bias against female children. Male children invariably tend to get away with most trespasses at home and society, unlike their female counterparts.

> *It has always baffled me why women ask for gender equality? Why do they want to settle for less? As Mother Nature has designed and empowered them, they are far superior to men in most areas. They must just rediscover themselves. They need not to copy men or be like men. The just need to be what they are by themselves. Salute to all women—the Saraswatis, the Durgas, the Maha Kaalis, and the Laxmis.*

Women Education

Education of mothers and older women is the key to eliminate prejudice against woman, otherwise feminism, as a reaction, will take its own toll on human happiness.

Let all mothers love and treat their daughters as they love and treat their sons, without bias or prejudice.

We humans must agree that women, after receiving equal opportunities, education and even otherwise, have undoubtedly proven to be equal or better than men in all walks of life. In practical terms, women are self-sufficient and do not really need men. So watch out, men!

Women are Not Material Commodities.

In India, which is home to about one-fifth of the human population, the traditional Hindu ritual of *kanya-daan* (donation of a daughter) at the time of wedding of their daughters is demeaning and detestable. The Indian government must abolish this term and the ritual associated with it in the same way as it recently banned the *triple-talaq* practice amongst the Muslim populace. Daughters are not material objects and can't be donated. No one, not even parents, have any right to do so.

Furthermore, in the Indian context, it is extremely degrading for daughters to be considered as *paraya-dhan* (wealth of strangers) by their parents, as they have been considered traditionally. They are not commodities; they are humans and, therefore, they too are children of their parents as are sons.

Toxic Social Divisions

Humanism binds humans; it is Divine. Humanism means having to treat every other human with respect, whilst upholding the intrinsic human dignity, and in the same manner as one would like to be treated in return by that human.

This world is pathetically divided along numerous lines—genders, religions, castes, ethnicities, skin colours, socio-economic classes, levels of education, professions, geographical regions etc. Has God divided this world? No, it is the humans who have divided this world for their selfish endeavours and to lord over other humans. Humans constantly endeavour to divide it further and keep looking for reasons to divide it more and more—it is always 'us' and 'them'; 'we' and 'they' etc.

Both feminism and misogyny are discriminatory, just like racism. Such behaviours reflect extremism; they are reactionary and prove to be potential sources of unhappiness and strife in our communities.

Both racism and gender bias are detestable, as both tend to break the natural human bond and the human spirit. To claim one's unequivocal or undisputed superiority over other humans, and then to discriminate or be prejudiced or biased against them, based on their looks, gender, skin colour, religion or caste, wealth, education, profession etc. is not only abhorrent or unethical but extremely sinful, in so far as the intrinsic respect and dignity of the humans is concerned.

Feminism Versus Gender Equality

Is gender equality compatible with the term 'feminism'? Is it possible to align these terms, without infringing on the traditional protocol and decency one must have towards females, and the intrinsic respect that they command and deserve? A friend, Dale Hartley, says:

"That depends what you mean by feminism. If you mean women making out men to be wrong in an attempt to guilt them into submission which some so-called feminists do, that is not feminism. That is an angry woman behaving as badly as the men she hates. If you mean women bonding together in the political struggle to gain equal treatment under the law; equal opportunity, education and treatment in life and the workplace; equal respect from society, and protection from male abuses where women are treated as property, as slaves, as objects of male sexual gratification, and as servants, to be abandoned, beaten or killed for disobedience or for just having a mind of their own. Then feminism is completely compatible with the idea of equality.

The problem in India from what I can see is there is a difference between what the law says and what society says. As a recent news report in India on the issue of women abandoning better paying jobs over legitimate concerns over their safety and their children's safety said "this country doesn't care for its wives and daughters." It's a statement that is hard to disagree with based on the evidence, and as men are the perpetrators, it is men who need to change their attitudes, and society which is currently controlled mostly by men that needs to confront how we are failing ourselves, the women in our lives and our society as a whole, by holding onto these bestial notions.

In Australia, we are further along in this conversation than India and much has been achieved, but I could not say this standard has yet been met. Old attitudes linger in the dark—but over time these are fluttering out like the dying flames of a fire that has burnt its fuel, as we realise as a society the overwhelming benefits for everyone, including men, of pursuing true equality."

This age-old matter needs a thorough and honest introspection by one and all. Our human race is still evolving; we still have a fair way to go before we achieve gender equilibrium. One extreme gives birth to another extreme—it takes a while before a sustainable middle ground is achieved. Thankfully, history bears witness that all issues finally achieve a resolution.

> *Equality and feminism are not about granting respect because of their gender but about not discriminating against someone because of their gender.*

Can Chivalry and Feminism Co-exist?

Chivalry and feminism are nonaligned, potentially on a collision course if one tries to align them. How can a body live if one of its parts fights with another part? They can't coexist; one has to give way to the other. But, on their own also, they are unstable, like a swinging pendulum. For a healthy human race, both must go.

All humans are born the same way, naked and crying; they go back to Mother Earth in not much different ways. Underneath that skin of ours, we all look same. So, who is superior? None, whosoever! Humans will continue to be primitive so long as they don't transcend all divisions created by them.

Humanism is what the world needs. Let us learn from the Buddha or from Gandhi or Martin Luther King Jr. So long as humans and what they do for a living are not respected, without bias or prejudice or discrimination, we humans will continue to contribute to human unhappiness and potential strife amongst communities. It will be always 'they' versus 'us'.

No human has the moral right to claim superiority over any other human on the planet. All humans are born equal. Respect one and all, but never prostrate before another person, whosoever he or she is. Also, never allow any human to prostrate before you or touch your feet. Never! A *namaskar* or a firm handshake will do, as equals. Namaskar means bowing to the Divinity in the other person, but never bowing to other person's adornments, ornaments, wealth, status or ego.

> *Let us promote equality amongst the humans and erase all division between them. Let us transcend all social barriers, outdated stigmas and religious ideologies that divide humans.*

Human Dignity and Civility

Civility defines a person. Difficult times test a person's character. A person's conduct in the face of provocation and adversity defines the person's upbringing, education and refinement. How a person behaves with one's rival, nemesis, enemy or a competitor during a face-off defines the humanness and dignity of that person. Upholding the inherent dignity of the other person is paramount and must never be forgotten even when the other person has completely contradictory beliefs on a subject or many subjects. One must fight the idea or the issue, whatever it is, but never the other person. Never make any argument or discussion personal.

Civility was well defined and exemplified during the dying moments of *Ravana*, the mighty king of Lanka, by *Lord Ram* when he asked his younger brother, *Lakshmana* (a known firebrand) to stand with hands folded near the former's feet (instead of head) and request him for some wise words.

Ravana was known to be a great learned person, a *maha-Pandit* (a great scholar). Lord Ram never lost respect for Ravana's personality, self-respect and knowledge, even though he fought him till the latter's death. Even in his victory, Lord Ram remained humble and dignified, and never ceased to be a good student. That is exactly what sports teach us—to be humble in our victory and dignified in our defeat. That is called the sportsman spirit—to take both loss and defeat in our stride. As per the Geneva Convention, army soldiers are trained to show respect to the mortal remains of the dead enemy soldiers. That is called civility. It is not only the respect towards the living; civility also means having to respect the dead.

Faith is Personal, Sacred

Faith is a very personal matter for every living individual on the planet. One must never challenge other people's faith. Faith is all what many people have that makes them stand upright and live through the struggles of their life. Our faith instils hope in us for a better tomorrow, and keeps us going. Faith and hope go together, they are intertwined.

People may belong to any religious group but their world of faith could possibly differ, depending upon their spirituality, upbringing, education, physical and mental health, and their social environment. Any mindless act of criticising and challenging other people's faith could be compared to an irresponsible act of stripping them naked, or removing the roof of their house, or making them orphans. Unnecessary criticism of religious faith of other people can be construed as an extremely reckless and provocative act, which potentially becomes a recipe for strife in communities, social disorder and even military conflicts.

Faith and Science

Students of science tend to irresponsibly challenge the faith of other people. It is akin to a knee-jerk reaction, possibly born out of their immaturity and shallow thinking. Such people try to replace a *religion of faith* with a *religion of science*, called scientism. Little do they realise that, as long as science is not able to conquer all diseases and death, people will cling to faith, whatever that is, such as worshiping a cow or praying to a tree.

Science is a tool, a mechanism, to uncover the mysteries of nature. Science is a pathway to discover the mysteries but may not be the final answer to all human pursuits and queries, especially about faith and complex human emotions—love, hate, anger, trust etc.

Faith

A person who does not respect one's own faith tends to disrespect the faith of other people. If you don't respect your own parents, others must not expect you to respect their parents either. One's faith is like one's parents, who are the first people in our life whom we trust blindly. Why? Because we have no other options; we are weak and feeble when we are born, and completely unable to help ourselves to survive in our early years. Our parents are our gods on earth.

> *The call of the hour is to recognise humanity and divinity in all humans. Let our individual faiths not divide us and make us less human or turn us against fellow humans of different faiths.*

Show-Off

There can be a thousand reasons to show-off—what we own or how we look—but it takes just one reason not to show-off, which is an ever-changing character of life.

Life is a great leveller, it takes back everything when our body dies, including all our pride and ego. Even the sun, the only visible god and the giver of life, does not show-off; it knows it will die one day.

Acknowledge and Thank the Human Endeavour

We thank God, whom no one has seen, when, in fact, we should acknowledge the human endeavour and thank those humans who go out of their way to help us, when we expect it least, or help us as part of their normal professional duty.

Many of us come across situations in our lives when we are extremely desperate and strangers unexpectedly appear out of nowhere and provide us with their timely assistance.

Recently, when the pilots of a Russian airliner landed their plane safely, on its belly in a corn field, after it was reported to be hit by birds, some people may have thanked God for saving all the lives aboard the plane. However, thankfully, many other people hailed the pilots as heroes and credited them with saving their precious lives.

If there would have been no survivors in the aforementioned plane crash, would the first group of people, who may have thanked God, accept the deaths as the will of God, or thanked God for causing the crash, or just kept quiet? Possibly, none of those! When lives are lost, people hunt for those responsible for causing deaths and demand severe punishment against them. No one person accepts such human losses as an Act of God, unless the deaths are caused by real acts of God, such as earthquakes, floods, cyclone, lightning bolts etc.

Human Hypocrisy

Many of us have faced situations in our lives when strangers have unexpectedly appeared to help us when we have felt desperate and hopeless. We call them angels from God. Can't we just call them humans? Are humans not supposed to be doing anything good? Why is God credited with doing good only and not causing any destruction and deaths? Are religions responsible for creating this skewed view against human nature?

It is human hypocrisy that makes us thank God for anything good that happens to us, rather than thank those who actually help us. We never blame God for bad things that happen to us. Instead, we hunt for the culprits and call for severe retribution against them.

Without the constant human endeavour over ages, we would still be living in the Stone Age, as hunters and gatherers. The day we realise this truth, we will rise above the religious divides and stop harassing and victimising humans belonging to other religions.

Humanism marks the ultimate human growth and progress. It is the highest religion we humans must strive for if we want to see real and sustainable peace on our earth.

Action and Not Just Talk

Important is what you are practically doing for the promotion of peace in the world. Are you striving to inculcate the universal human values in yourself and other people around you? Are you striving to be a good human being or a good religious person?

If talks, wishes and thinking positive were sufficient, we would not have to go out, earn money and look after our families. Our children would not go to school to receive education if we did not pay for their education. Food would not grow all by itself unless millions of farmers and other people worked hard on the ground and produced, transported and sold it to us.

A country would not be protected from external threats if all people just prayed to God and if soldiers did not leave their homes to stand guard at its borders, in extreme harsh environmental and geographical conditions, and sacrificed their lives when required. Our selfless actions matter. What we think or wish or pray doesn't make any positive difference in the world. Give your best to the world, in your own little, humble capacity. Every human is gifted, by nature, with a unique gift. Use that gift in a timely manner to make a positive difference in the world and endeavour to leave a positive impact on the humanity in your lifetime before you finally disappear.

The Bhagwad Gita is all about selfless actions. It is absolutely not about watching, as a passive witness, the wrongs done by others. In no case, it is about ritualistic prayers, ritualistic ceremonies or any theoretical talk.

Bribery is Theft

Bribery is akin to stealing; it is an act of theft. A society that does not see the act of bribery as an act of stealing and theft can be termed as a society of thieves and robbers. A person who demands or receives an undue favour or a bribe—whether monetary or sexual or in kind or of any other nature—from another person, in lieu of rendering any routine service or assistance for which the person receives a salary from one's employer, is nothing short of a thief or a robber.

The disease of stealing lies very much in the mindset of people. It is a psychological disorder. Alarmingly, people who indulge in bribery—taking and giving—try to even bribe God as an act of reconciliation and self-cleansing. A portion of the stolen money is offered in secret and in not-so-secret, donations and offerings to God in temples and other places of worship. There is nothing glorifying about it. It is a shameful situation.

To change a society for the better, its children must be holistically educated and firmly made to realise that an act of bribery is akin to an act of stealing or robbery, just like what a robber or a thief does. Strict punitive measures are a must to check this menace, but that requires brave people of conscience and character at all levels. Law & order should be just, efficient, honest and timely.

Rape is the Highest Crime Against Humanity

Many people call for the death sentence as legal punishment for criminals who commit rape. In this regard, the following six important aspects need very careful consideration if death sentence were to become law, given its seriously irreversible consequences, and if it were to serve as an effective deterrent:

- The case must be dealt with extreme urgency by a specially trained police squad, under the jurisdiction of special courts.
- To attract punishment, the crime must be proven *beyond doubt* otherwise the law has the potential to be abused or misused for a range of social reasons.
- False accusations must carry equally exemplary severe punishment, such as a minimum life-term jail sentence and a hefty monetary fine.
- Once proven *beyond doubt*, the convicted rapist must be punished at the earliest possible.
- Most importantly, the punishment must also serve as an effective deterrent against future rapes by unsuspecting individuals. As such, the death sentence on its own may not be an effective deterrent. The punishment must be made psychologically painful and socially shameful as well.

> *Exemplary punishment of some proven convicted criminals—to instil extreme fear in potential criminals—is the need of the hour to deter this heinous crime against humanity.*

Self-Management on Social Media

When we differ from other people in our viewpoints on social media, we have only three options:

(1) Respond politely, as an educated person, with utmost civility and respect for the intrinsic human dignity, without making any personal, derogatory attacks on the other person.
(2) Remain quiet unless it is unbearable to do so; and
(3) Unfriend the other person.

Some people throw all the mud they can without exercising any self-restraint, which is extremely uncivil and unbecoming of any educated community. Our response defines our culture and class. It reflects who we are. There are many who judge us based on how we respond in situations of provocation and personal attack.

Voice of an Indian Taxi Driver

Early morning on 4 July 2018, after landing in New Delhi, I happened to hear the thoughts of my cab driver (Bhagirath, 50) during my 45-minute journey from Terminal 3 (IGIA) to Greater Noida. I was sitting on the front passenger seat and eager to trigger a meaningful conversation with the driver. This habit not only highlights the dignity of work and labour, but also demonstrates respect for the intrinsic human dignity.

We must treat all our service-providers as we wish to be treated by them. No one person becomes big or small based on the nature of one's work; all humans are born equal and command respect. We become small only when we discriminate, consciously or otherwise, against other people based on their calling, colour, social status, religion or caste.

Bhagirath asked me to publish his following thoughts:

- *Expensive private education*: He demands a high quality, but affordable, education for all poor masses. He complained against the mushrooming growth of private educational institutions that fleece poor people.
- *Dowry*: He said, as his daughter's wedding would potentially cost him up to about Rupees 5 Lakhs, he is not in a position to marry her off, as he can't afford her dowry. He wants that

the State should introduce the Anti-dowry Act and make dowry illegal, with severe punitive measures against those people who offer and/or demand a dowry, irrespective of their social status.

- *Caste-based selection of electoral candidates*: He said all candidates must be selected based on their educational background, and not their caste.
- *Reservations*: He maintains the Indian system of *reservations* is unfair and, therefore, wants it to be scrapped completely. Instead, people should be assisted financially based on only their household income. He wants that all poor people—from all backgrounds/castes/religions—should be able to receive the State assistance through a means-tested social security system.
- *Different laws*: He demands *one common law* for all Indians, irrespective of religion or caste.
- *Reservations-based teacher appointment*: He wants all teachers should be appointed based on only their teaching capability and educational merit, and not *reservations*.
- *Subsidised gas cylinders based on reservations*: He said this practice is unfair and should be stopped. Instead, gas cylinders should be provided based on only the household income.
- *Availability of ration cards to only some people*: He demands ration cards should be made available to all poor people and not only some privileged sections of the community.

In addition to the above, he also made the following useful suggestions:

- Streams and rivulets should be connected with main rivers, so that rainwater is not wasted. Through the construction of dams over these streams and rivers, greater access for water will be available to numerous farmers for farming use.

- Driver licenses should be linked with Aadhar card. Also, *Batch licenses* should be introduced in all states; otherwise middlemen exploit the system and fleece the drivers who move from one state to the other.
- Sale of land—residential, commercial and agricultural—should be linked with Aadhar card.
- Good quality government hospitals and degree level colleges should be opened in all districts, so that people don't have to travel long distance to access these facilities.
- Survey of agricultural land should be undertaken on a regular basis, as the population increases. He does not recall any survey undertaken in his living memory.

In his own words, Bhagirath[2] is not an educated person.

Indian taxi drivers provide an invaluable firsthand insight into the country's general health and the mindset of common people in regard to the state of affairs of the country—liveability, health and happiness, culture and values, political infrastructure and governance.

Indian street vendors, rickshaw pullers, coolies, labourers and domestic helpers work in very challenging conditions, on the open roads (the blood vessels of a country), and not in air-conditioned offices. These people don't rely on the social media or the mass electronic media for knowing the country's general health. Interestingly, but not surprisingly, they form the bulk of the voters. As their opinion counts, one must listen to them.

Humanism

The call of the hour is to recognise humanity and divinity in all humans. Let our individual faiths not divide us and make us less human or turn us against fellow humans of different faiths.

2 Bhagirath Prasad Kushwa comes from a farming community from Jharkhand. He hails from Gram Kadidih, Post Office Padariya, Thana Markaccho, Zila Kodarma.

The human race has progressed solely based on its consistent, selfless, positive endeavours, to support life, over the last 200,000 years. The bright, positive human side, as a natural law, prevails over its dark, negative side. Humans come in with all kinds of mindsets, some as angels, who strive to heal and stitch wounds together.

Jacinda Ardern, New Zealand's PM, represents the best of human race and people's leadership. Leading from the front, with empathy, compassion and benevolence, she got the gun law passed in just six days.

Bond with other people to save the world and humanity. Build common threads and don't look for differences, otherwise you may possibly tear it apart. Bond with others by finding, recognising and feeding the common threads between humans. Weave those threads into a global humane network. You may possibly tear apart the whole world if you look only at the differences between you and others.

We are flowers of one garden. Let us live in peace and harmony. We have a benevolent Gardener. Our sky is blue; our land is green and gold. Our red land up north (in Australia) is our wealth. If we sincerely commit ourselves to do our bit for the good of humanity every day, we will find no time to waste in any social gossip and we will be much happier. A country will be happy, sustainable and invincible only if she respects and properly treats her farmers, soldiers and teachers.

Let us act as soldiers of peace and happiness. Let us try to make this world a better place. Let us try to bring smiles and joy to our fellow humans wherever they are, in person or through the web, including our family, colleagues, friends, neighbours, clients and vendors, co-passengers and strangers equally. Only when we help others unselfishly, we can be truly happy.

My heart cries but God is silent. They were humans. They were bowing to God in their prayers when they were gunned down. They did not know their killer. My heart cries, it bleeds. (On the Christchurch massacre, 2019)

My heart cries. They were humans. They were returning to work after meeting their families. They had just hugged their parents, siblings, wives and children. They had promised them they would be home soon. And they were blown away. They did not know their killers. My heart cries, it bleeds. (Referring to the Pulwama car-bomb blast, 2019)

My heart cries. They were humans. They had to leave their homes where their ancestors had lived and died. Many of their sons, daughters, fathers and grandfathers were gunned down. They did not know their killers. My heart cries, it bleeds. (On exiled Pandits of Kashmir, 1990) My heart cries. They were humans. Tens of millions died in wars and millions in natural disasters. They did not know their killers. My heart cries, it bleeds.

God you have never cried, you have never spoken. You will never cry or speak in the future too. Why do we call your name in vain, why do we fight in your name?

It was a beautiful but much simpler world. My imagination and thinking capacity grew, as I enjoyed my own company watching the snow fall. (My childhood in Kashmir, pre-1990)

Unless the global focus shifts towards bringing out and promoting the oneness of the human race rather than highlighting and feeding its surficial differences, the world will never see peace. A deliberate violent attack on people of one religion—any religion—is an attack on the whole humanity. Cool heads, and not violent reactions, are the need of the hour.

All humans must strive for humanity. Let us all pledge that we shall together fight against such barbaric and heartless acts of terrorism as the one that has shocked New Zealand and the wider world. (On the Christchurch massacre, 2019) Revenge and retribution are not in my nature. There are numerous people who don't like me and there are some I don't like, and that is all human. I prefer to leave them alone to fight their own day to day battles of life and survival, as I fight my own. Why should we hurt one another? Let us be civil. Contemplation and self-reflection will heal each one of us. One day, all of us will be just stories, and perhaps not even that.

It is nice to be proud about your nation but it would be nicer to be

However, the reality is that each one of us responds differently to the rises and falls in our lives; some lose their head whereas some remain grounded at all times. No two people emerge the same from a common adversity; one remains stuck forever to the past, while as the other undergoes an accelerated growth spurt. William Shakespeare—in his play, *As You like It*—uplifts us as follows:

> *Sweet are the uses of adversity, which, like the toad, ugly and venomous, wears yet a precious jewel in his head …*

Differential Human Growth

Life reveals its mysterious shades in so many mysterious ways. How often do we see a person who, despite his personal suffering, suffers—spiritually and mentally—for the people who may have caused or contributed to the reason—directly or directly—of his suffering? People generally remain tied to their past misfortunes because their past wounds—psychological and physical—may be too deep to heal in one lifetime; or they constantly nourish their past wounds with painful memories; or they keep wishing for retribution. And they may not be blamed; they are just poor humans—herd animals, not angels. Most people cling to the memories of their past personal suffering, they nourish vengeful wishes that greater suffering befall their former adversaries. Wishful thoughts of revenge cloud their mind and the ability to think with prudence.

But, life kneads and moulds each one of us differently. There must be many people and, in fact, there are many people who do manage to transcend common human frailties and do suffer immensely for the same very people against whom they may have serious past grievances.

Although this may sound oxymoronic, nonsensical or weird to many people, a question still arises: 'What makes such people suffer for their past adversaries?' The answer could be perhaps that their past suffering may have churned them enough to the extent it has brought out the best in them and purged their soul of anger, hate, ill-will and retribution; perhaps their empathy far exceeds their personal suffering; perhaps they don't want the history to repeat itself; or perhaps they understand that forgiveness is the best medicine for self-healing and liberation of the soul from karmic cycles of perpetual pain and suffering.

Such people never rejoice in the suffering of other people, let alone the suffering of the people who share a common ancestry with them, those who are born from their soil, eat their food and speak their language.

Now, what do we do with these empathetic people? Should they be crucified? Are they sinners?

- Should the emotional response of empathetic people be considered socially unacceptable and politically blasphemous?
- Does empathy make one weak?
- Does compassion make one a coward?
- Should people with empathy and compassion be considered lesser humans?
- Are forgiveness and empathy not acceptable if shown towards one's *perceived* adversaries?
- Are humans meant to be unforgiving and revengeful towards their *perceived* adversaries?
- Is nourishing and exhibiting an animalistic sense of retribution necessary to qualify one as a 'normal' person?

If the general answer to all above questions is *yes*, the world has undoubtedly not understood Gautama Buddha and Jesus Christ, both messengers of peace and forgiveness. Are we still living in the medieval ages despite looking educated, sophisticated and civilised? Are our civilised words hollow? Our suffering should have normally helped us to grow but, sadly, that does not happen with many of us.

Our past may be full of wrongs—for and against us—but prudence demands our present must be saved from more wrongs being committed if peace is allowed to prevail, or else the cycle of pain will keep moving perpetually. Two wrongs never make one right.

Anything that one would not wish to go through oneself must never be unleashed on others or even entertained as a thought. Do unto others what you wish for yourself. Your actions will return to you with multipliers. Never forget that, at the end of the day, each one of us will return to the earth as a mere handful of dust, sans our pride.

Freedom

Humans strive for freedom—of expression, thought and action—which must be considered as a matter of our birthright provided, of course, our freedom does not trespass or infringe upon the freedom of our fellow beings. Humans—poor or rich, uneducated or educated—are born with an intrinsic expectation to be respected. Active listening reflects one of the most important aspects of respect that we can show towards the other person. Where a government does not listen the public, it loses their respect, faith and trust. Where parents don't listen to their children, they effectively lose them; children turn rebellious as soon as they grow up. If parents try to confine their children against their will, government takes them away, at least in the civilised world. It is never an internal matter for anyone—an individual or a family or an organisation or any government—when it is a matter that concerns human beings. Even attempt to commit suicide is considered a serious criminal offence in all countries, carrying a jail term, and so are the acts of abortion and euthanasia in many countries.

If humans can't enjoy free will and absolute control over themselves, how can they claim to have absolute freedom to control and restrain other people against their will? Matters concerning human beings are never an internal matter for any family, organisation or a country; a number of world organisations do maintain a very close vigil.

One needs to have a good heart to be able to connect with another good heart. Broken, sad hearts are potential seeds of greater sadness for the wider world. Our political head tends to mislead us in the matters of heart. Similarly, trust is not a matter of right, it is earned painstakingly over long periods of time, with goodwill and sincerity; however, it takes just one wrong act—of lie and deceit—to lose it. One must be genuine so as to receive genuine hugs from others. One must be sincere before expecting sincerity from other people.

A piece of land without happy people living on it is as good as dead. It may have strategic importance and perhaps may also be a source of natural resources but sooner or later it will become a significant source of unrest and instability for its owners. If a land is to be won, its people must also be won. If people are to be won, their hearts must be won. Force does not win hearts.

Human Degradation

History is full of examples of authoritarian, repressive and dictatorial regimes that caused significant damage to the very country they ruled. The present is witnessing an ominous trend of political trickery and subterfuge across the globe. Political and social sophistication, decorum and protocol—which one reads about in the school books—seem to be fast fading to a distant past. Social media and electronic mass media are tactfully abused, by authoritarian regimes and compromised (flawed) democracies, for undertaking political chicanery.

A political act that alienates others and leaves deep, painful, and permanent, generational memories in them is never worth undertaking. Pressure-cooker situations must be avoided in all cases, especially if the pressure-valve is kept closed. Humans behave as springs, the more they are compressed, and the more is the ferocity with which they recoil.

A common person is tricked into seeing and believing in a mirage—something that does not exist. Fear psychosis is used to manipulate people; so are false promises and hollow incentives. The common man has been made to suffer from an incurable disease of illusion, rather delusion in most cases. People regurgitate what they are fed day and night through social media and the power-controlled mass media.

The so-called educated people seem to have lost common sense, independent thoughts and the ability to think critically. Blissfully, some of those who can't read or write—and don't have access to social media—may be able to retain some degree of common sense and perhaps also the gift of independent thinking. Ethical and moral degradation, reflected by a blatant use of misleading lies and might, seems to have become an accepted order of the day.

Consequences

Those who nurture the seeds of retribution and revenge, for whatever reason, legitimate or not, actually nurture the seeds of doom and death. They get imprisoned in a perpetual cycle of suffering. They don't realise their liberation actually lies in their forgiveness of their adversaries—real or perceived.

These days, it is not very easy to see a friend from a foe, or decide what is genuine and what is not. Our world seems to be messed up, by us alone. Perhaps we are too many people on this planet, all fighting for survival. Our population has multiplied more than 7 times in the past 400 years and in the next three decades, the multiplier is expected to shoot up to 9.5. Our demands far exceed our natural resources. We have become *civilised predators*. We survive by encroaching on one another's space—physical, mental and spiritual. Our predatory growth is not sustainable; Nature will work through us and cut down our numbers significantly. We will fight war; we will see death and devastation all around us.

It will be appropriate to end this article with a quote from Mark Twain:

> *It ain't what you don't know that gets you into trouble. It's what you know for sure that just ain't so.*

Only when we are filled with empathy, compassion and care for our fellow beings, and all other life forms, should we be entitled to call ourselves humans, otherwise there is not much difference between us two-legged beings and other four-legged beings whom we call animals. Let us be humans, once again; let us treat other humans as humans, once again. Let us grow and transcend all divisions amongst humans! Can we finally be humans, again? If not, we should stop calling ourselves humans.

One who derives pleasure in the suffering of another person has fallen spiritually. One who justifies such pleasure has fallen both morally and ethically. One who justifies and legitimises the suffering of another person has fallen as a human. How can we see peace if we keep nourishing the seeds of revenge and hate in our hearts? History repeats itself.

My Friends and My Foes

I can't see my friends from my foes; they all look same, my friends and my foes.
Some give me joy and some give me purpose, my friends and my foes.
I can't hate my friends, I can't hate my foes; they are all like me, my friends and my foes.
Who is mine and who is not; they are all for themselves, my friends and my foes.
We are all mortals and we all will be stories one day, my friends and my foes.
I am my friend and I am my foe, I must look within myself for my friends and my foes.

Girl education...

Global education should make complete, noble, good human beings

SIX

EDUCATION

Building World-Class Educational Institutions

THE STATUS QUO of higher education industry around the world changes rapidly due to the challenges that it keeps facing due to the ongoing new global challenges. The elite higher education institutions are forced to think globally and develop a strong student and a wider stakeholder value proposition so that they can differentiate themselves from their competitors.

At an international conference in India, in late August 2019, a number of eminent educationists from India and overseas presented their views on *how to build world-class institutions in India*, with particular reference to tertiary education. Interestingly, there is no one definition of a *world-class institution*. The eminent speakers believed the provision of the following abilities, as a minimum, were essential for any institution to be called a world-class institution.

- An encouraging environment for research
- Work experience and volunteering opportunities
- Opportunities for international experiences

- Links with industry partners and professional bodies
- Incubator facilities and engages with start-up communities
- Extracurricular activities for holistic development

A Philosophical Perspective

Logically, the purpose of world-class institutions must be to produce world-class citizens, and not those close-minded, world-haters. Therefore, for creating world-class institutions, world-class humans are required to run them and world-class humans are required to learn and teach there. One may ask, "What does that mean?" The answer to this simple, innocent question leads to a pathway of creating world-class institutions; however, the answer may also be potentially challenging, rather confronting, to a polarised mind, living in a capitalistic community, with a nationalistic bent of mind.

What do we understand by the term *world-citizen*?

- A world citizen is expected to regard people of all nations, ethnic communities, religious faiths, genders and sexual orientations equally, with dignity and respect, without bias and discrimination.
- The world citizen may act locally, but must accept being globally responsible. In doing so, the person must remain aware about all pertinent global issues in view, such as the environment and sustainability, global peace, human and natural resources etc.
- The world citizen must humbly acknowledge and respect the inputs made by humans from across the globe, past and the present—in all fields of learning—science and technology, medicine, mathematics, literature, arts and humanities—without trying to be overly boisterous and proud about the local input.
- The world citizen must never stop being a student even after achieving the highest possible professional or academic level.
- The world citizen must transcend all man-made divisions—national boundaries, religious faiths, socio-economic

hierarchy—in order to gain a world view and be able to cater to the demands of the world.

- The world citizen must understand that it is not very important what kind of work one does but how does one do what one does. A conceptual understanding of this mantra will help to inculcate a sense of respect in the person for all kinds of works and workers, develop respect for human dignity and labour. Unless this happens, a community will never witness human development, thus undermining the core purpose of education. Unless humans develop, communities will never be happy and progressing. Social hierarchy caused by socio-economic divisions, driven by class, wealth and power, acts against overall community wellbeing.

World Rankings

Based generally on their attributes, universities are ranked on a number of systems, including:

- QS World University Ranking
- Times Higher Education World University Ranking (THEWUR)
- Academic Ranking of World Universities (ARWU)

No Indian university figures on the list of the world's top 200 universities in 2019.

As per an article by Forbes, dated 10 August 2009, *What Makes a University Great*, the following three factors separated the top international universities from the rest:

- Talented dedicated teachers, researchers and students; Open-minded, bright and talented faculty and students from across the globe.
- Several sources of funding: Government funding for operational spending and research; contract research funding from public organisations and private firms, and earnings from endowments, gifts and tuition fees.

- Freedom, autonomy and leadership: Unrestrained scientific inquiry, critical thinking, innovation and creativity, without external bureaucratic and political influences.

Desirable Academic Virtues

- Freedom to purse truth: Scholars have the necessary freedom to pursue truth.
- Freedom to pursue all ideas: Scholars can pursue a full range of ideas—popular and unpopular, familiar and novel, probable and improbable.
- Respect for knowledge and expertise: Expert knowledge is valued and respected by students and faculty.
- Respect and value for creativity and innovation: Acquired knowledge is respected and the intellectual skills, gifts are valued; individuals can challenge existing beliefs and develop new ideas and understanding.
- Merit is rewarded: Rewards and success depend solely on the academic merit, and one's commitment and capacity to do the work.
- Inclusiveness: Membership not reserved based on gender, race or ethnicity, religion, socio-economic hierarchy or any other personal characteristics.

Investment in the Foundations

At a conference, only one young speaker (frustratingly) emphasised the need to invest in the foundations of the educational infrastructure, i.e. the quality of education received by students at the pre-primary and primary school levels before world-class institutions can be made. And he was so very right; he may have nailed the issue right on its head. He spoke in Hindi to vent his frustration.

For higher learning, importance of independent, critical thinking—with an open mind, as required for undertaking genuine research, and not through plagiarism, at tertiary level—can never be over-emphasised. Unless this essential art of learning is inculcated in young minds, particularly in the first ten years of their life, quality, cutting-edge research is not generally possible at the later stages of education. Young minds must be encouraged to fearlessly ask questions—why, how, when, where—and not be reprimanded for doing so by their pre-primary and primary school teachers, or by their parents, particularly if their parents claim to be educated.

Only when the young minds are allowed to think independently and develop an open mind and the art of critical thinking, the foundations of an educational system can be deemed to be sound. For sound foundations, therefore, the educators that deal with young minds must be specialised in the art of teaching pre-primary and primary school students, and considered as professionals, similar to engineers, doctors or lawyers. Most importantly, the educators must be amongst the brightest minds and remunerated at the highest possible professional levels. Whilst it may help to call an institution world-class from materialistic and business point of view, any institution that develops world-class citizens, as defined above—with holistic, global education—can be practically considered as a world-class institution. On the basis of the above, in the Indian context, the role of National Council of Educational Research and Teaching (NCERT) acquires an extremely high importance with regard to laying the foundations of the educational infrastructure across the country, which is necessary for the construction of a vibrant, research-oriented tertiary educational infrastructure. NCERT has, therefore, an essential role to play in shaping the destiny of the country.

The preaching of politicians has made our masses believe that their country is the greatest country in the world, with a proud and illustrious history and a rich culture. They claim the developed world has used the wisdom of the scientists and mathematicians of our land from a distant past and yet they struggle to figure out how to build world-class educational institutions. They are actually striving to build the beyond-world-class institutions.

As long as people are gripped by nationalism and pride, and believe the rest of the world is their enemy and trying to undermine their country, they can never produce world citizens needed to build world-class institutions. An attempt to make world-class institutions in a country that claims to be the greatest country in the world is simply oxymoronic and practically self-defeating.

Limitations of Education

One would assume that education would solve all issues in the world, but does it? It seems to work both ways, depends upon who is using it.

Knowledge is power and, therefore, must be imparted and used judiciously, with extreme caution, by the educators and the students. On one hand, thankfully, it empowers the female gender, which has been openly discriminated against for centuries—socially, culturally and religiously—as well as the poor and the socially disadvantaged people. It illuminates ones mind and removes ignorance, thereby empowering it. However, on the other hand, it also empowers the dangerous and destructive minds—the villains—in this world.

In this day and age, most strife, war mongering, and propagation of social hate and violence is generally the brain-child of the so-called educated people. It would be wrong to say that most educated people are corrupt, but it would not be far from the truth that most corrupt people are educated, some very well educated. In fact, there could be an alarmingly direct correlation between the level of education and the level of corruption.

Corruption at high levels requires only the educated people, with full know-how of internal working, loopholes and the escape routes. So, from that point of view, it does not really matter if the person has the *educated* label or not; what matters is what kind of education the person has received. Has the education made the person peace-loving, benevolent, happy and positive or if it is the other way round?

Education Works Both Ways

Like many things in life, education and knowledge work both ways—for the benefit of humanity and against it—depending upon the intention of the user. Technological knowledge is used both ways, as a facility but also a means of destruction and devastation. A medicine also proves to be a poison if misused or abused. If and when used properly and judiciously, knowledge and technology prove to be beneficial for mankind. However, when misused, they have disastrous consequences.

- Food is important for survival, but excess of it makes one a glutton, and potentially obese and morbidly sick.
- Water is a life saver but it can also drown a person.
- Sugar, when consumed in a limited quantity, makes desserts delicious; but, in a large quantity, it is nothing short of a white poison that potentially kills through diabetes, cancer and a range of deadly diseases.
- Medicines cure us when used as per the doctor's recommended use and dosage. But, when misused, they have the opposite consequences.
- Many insomniac people need sleeping tablets to fall into slumber, but many people also commit suicide by overdosing themselves.
- Radioactive materials can be used for curing sick people, as well as for making nuclear bombs.
- A knife that helps in the kitchen can also be used to kill.
- Motor vehicles and aeroplanes, until recently, considered to be such great facilities for commuting, are now also being used as weapons of mass destruction.
- Fire is used for cooking but, when uncontrolled, it can reduce everything to ashes.

One Type of Education Does Not Fit All

One type of education does not fit all minds. It does not make any sense to empower a person with a certain skill set or a technology or a certain domain of knowledge if that person has the intent to cause harm to others. Such a person needs holistic education (moral, civil, ethical, and environmental) that transforms him/her completely at his/her core, for the benefit of the world at large.

Many people mask their negative thoughts and evil plans easily. Such people can't be identified till they commit violent acts; for example, the mass shootings that happen in the US on a regular basis are committed by seemingly quiet people. Therefore, education must be *holistic* for all, without taking any chances, as there are no labels on the foreheads of people that can identify them. The assumption must be that all students can potentially develop negative and destructive tendencies; therefore, before that happens, their minds must be holistically developed.

When an education system is seen to be a mechanism mainly for gaining material wealth and winning competitions and forging ahead of others, it can be considered to have lost its primary objective. It makes selfish, unhappy and mean individuals. Such a rotten education system must be scrapped altogether, sooner than later, otherwise it will further exacerbate a growing strife and unhappiness in the world. The world urgently requires holistic education for one and all, for complete human development, where humans enjoy the logical end-product of life—i.e. good health (mental, spiritual, physical), peace and happiness. Our world does not need education for (hollow) materialistic progress of unhappy and potentially violent individuals.

Education and India

Unless the total mindset, concept, mechanism and infrastructure of education changes urgently in India, the country will never attain pure happiness and real human progress. Corruption, fragmentation and human exploitation will grow unabated. Education must be seen as a service and not as a cash-cow industry.

The performance of engineers can be judged by the end-users of the products (structures) they design and construct. The performance of doctors can be judged by the pace and degree of recovery of their patients. The performance of leaders can be gauged based on the health and happiness of the nation and all its citizens, especially the women. Similarly, the performance of teachers and educators can be judged based on the degree of benevolence of the young citizens they produce in the schooling system.

Just the way the strength and integrity of the foundation of a building is essential for its desired performance, holistic education in primary schools is essential for laying the foundations of character building of young citizens. Therefore, primary schooling must be of the highest standard, free, compulsory and holistic. Primary school teachers must be amongst the brightest minds, dedicated to serve the nation and, in return, remunerated at the highest salary levels.

Educators and policy makers in India, are you listening?

One's class, wealth, position, power or education doesn't make one wise, refined, reformed, humble or emancipated. These virtues are precious gifts from nature. One can't buy, learn or acquire them. Material detachment and humility may be two of the doorways to receive them from nature. Why have not all the rich and educated people made real human progress? Why don't wealth and education make all people wise?

> *If educated and influential families don't take the lead as social reformers, then who will? Is social reform meant only for others? Should the social reformists not practice social reform before they preach them to others?*

Right to Vote & Right to Education in India

In India, voting rights must be linked with the completion of basic school education, at least Class 10th, and the prospective voters must be required to attend school from the age of 6 up to at least the age of 16 before they are provided with the voter's card. The reason being, in parliamentary democracies, as the people's representatives are chosen by the majority vote, it is important that the votes are cast by the people who are educated and informed enough to ascertain the background and integrity of politicians who claim to represent them. It is not uncommon to see many dim-witted politicians addressing large election rallies. From their appearances and facial expressions, one can easily imagine the (poor) educational background of the people sitting on the ground in those rallies. Such people can be easily deceived and exploited by many slimy sweet-talking politicians.

Literacy Versus Education in India

On paper, India's literacy rate is reported to be around 75%. Interestingly, how is the term 'literacy' defined in India? Is it the ability to write one's name in an Indian language or ability to read and write at a certain meaningful level? As per the census data of 2015, and with reference to the following links, only 4.5% of the population in India was university graduate or above.

To ensure a vibrant democracy and prevent the exploitation of the poor and the illiterate—by mainly the politicians, the wealthy and the influential—and more importantly, to bring about equality amongst all her citizens, India needs to sincerely enforce the Right to Education Act (RTE) in letter and spirit to allow equal opportunities for all her children and generate equity across her society—the poor and the rich, and across all gender groups.

India needs firm implementation of the RTE with an aggressive educational campaign to:

- Make unequal societies equal to the limit possible.
- Stop exploitation of the poor and the illiterate by more affluent and literate sections of the society.
- Break down the societal snobbery of the rick and influential.
- Break down the silos in which people live and operate.
- Let the lower socio-economic sections of the community come up the societal ladder via education, entrepreneurship and regular jobs, like in the west. Why can't the rich and more educated people work for themselves, like their counterparts in the west? Why do they need domestic 'slaves' to work for them?
- Restore gender equity, which is a must in order to:
  - ➢ Stop female foeticide
  - ➢ Restore dignity of all women
  - ➢ Get rid of all the regressive societal ills and bad social

practices/taboos/stigmas due to the ignorance and exploitation of women

- Stop mindless population growth

All women must have the equal opportunity and the skills to work professionally outside their home, like their male counterparts, instead of staying at home and serving as children-producing factories.

Poor Educational Infrastructure in India

Given that about 70 percent population lives in rural and backward areas, one can easily argue that more than 70 percent children in India are marginalised based on where they are born—urban or rural areas—and the family they are born to—educated and rich, or uneducated and poor? A person's background dictates that person's opportunities for undertaking high school and tertiary education. People of poorer background become vulnerable for exploitation by the richer and higher educated people, and keep languishing indefinitely in the lower socio-economic communities.

On paper now, the Indian Constitution provides free and compulsory education for children between the ages of 6 and 14, with an aim to bring out-of-school children, particularly those from the disadvantaged groups and those with disabilities, into the formal education system. However, due to poor implementation of the RTE Act, all children are not in the schools.

Due to poor educational infrastructure in government schools—shortage of teachers, shortage of civil infrastructure (buildings, facilities, electricity and water), poor governance, poor learning environment etc. especially in the rural areas, where more than 70 percent Indians live, the enrolment of children is not 100 percent. Even for those students who are enrolled, the quality of education received is poor.

Although the elementary school education is the state responsibility, as per the RTE Act, this responsibility is being shifted by the government to private organisations that run schools for profit. The current system, thus, promotes the growth of private schools. The elementary education and, thereafter, the opportunities in life are, therefore, monopolised by the children of the relatively richer communities. In a nutshell, the current educational system in India, instead of eliminating inequalities, is further exacerbating the factors that lead to inequality amongst its citizens.

To ensure a homogenous and educated community, which can respect and work with one another, aggressive enforcement of the RTE is a must. After all, all humans are born equal. Then, why should one enjoy more privileges than the other just because one is born in a more privileged community.

How silly is it to undertake patchy repairs and expensive upgradation works in the superstructure of a house whose foundations have weakened significantly over years of deliberate neglect? Shockingly, the owner of the house is constructing more rooms in the same house to accommodate more family members. If the foundations of this house are not urgently treated and adequately strengthened, a total collapse of this house is imminent. The Indian education system needs a complete overhaul and not patchy repairs.

Education is Seen as a Business in India

In a country like India, education must not be seen as business by private organisations. Of course, they can contribute but the system needs to be more regulated by the government so that the overall objectives of the RTE are met without being a subject of financial affordability of the citizens.

Private education encourages formation of unequal societies, with children coming from expensive private schools turning into social snobs as they grow up. This dents the respect for inherent human dignity and the dignity of work itself. Humans and works are classified as 'superior' and 'inferior' based on the educational background and wealth of the individuals. Discrimination of humans based on their wealth and calling can be construed as blasphemous on both moral and spiritual grounds.

To bring equality across all her societies, government must build more schools, with adequate number of qualified permanent teachers, especially in the rural and backward areas. Bright minded teachers, with attractive remuneration and facilities, should be attracted towards the government schooling system for working in the rural and backward areas. All teachers must be appraised regularly for their performance.

Enforcement of Education

For enforcement of the RTE, parents who don't send their children to school must face several punitive actions, enforced by a joint task force led by the education and the policing departments. One way could be that such parents potentially lose the custody of the child to the state, such as in Australia. Second way could be sterilisation of both parents to prevent them from having any more children.

If you can't take care of your children and give them the RTE, you can't have them too. You also forfeit the right to produce any more children. Extraordinary situations warrant extraordinary solutions for India, a country of 1.37 billion souls and an ever increasing population. It is a country that grows and consumes much beyond her means. In India, education typically means achieving general literacy, rote learning and acquiring some general knowledge. Unfortunately, critical thinking and philosophy are not encouraged. As such, children don't learn the art of thinking outside the box.

In the 70s and 80s of Kashmir, and perhaps in the rest of the country, school learning generally meant memorising lessons. Rote learning, and not acquiring the basic understanding of the subject matter, was the order of the day. A student was expected to reproduce exactly what the teacher (or tutor) had written on the blackboard in the classroom to maximise the examination score (marks). The emphasis was mostly laid on acquiring the General Knowledge—such as 'who is who', historical dates and other statistics—and not on instilling the habit of critical thinking, through philosophy. I'm not sure if this has changed over time.

> *Education is the key to the human progress. More women than men are at the forefront of research in education, including STEM education. Men are left behind to play the supporting roles. Well done, women!*

Engineering Surrounds us Like Air

The way air surrounds us but we don't see it till it moves as a gentle breeze or as wind, or is polluted, we remain unaware of the world around us that has been created by engineers from all streams of the engineering profession. As we depend on clean air and water for our survival, our life also depends heavily on the robust work done by engineers from all streams.

We don't normally appreciate what engineers do till our life moves smoothly and without a hiccup. Only when a building or a bridge falls, or a machine fails, or a power failure occurs and disrupts our normal life, we become aware about this reality of our modern life.

Engineering is a creative process, so it can be construed as a creative art. An engineer turns into a number-crunching mathematician when he/she loses the sense of creativity and imagination. The word 'engineering' comes from the word 'ingenuity'. Engineers and architects use known and established scientific laws (physics and chemistry) and mathematical principles in their work.

The word 'architect' comes from the word 'arch'. An architect conceives the shape and size, as well as the aesthetic/architectural features of a structure based on its theme, objectivity and functionality—residential, commercial, industrial, art, educational etc.

> *Engineering is about thinking outside the box and putting an idea safely into a functional shape.*

Geotechnical Engineering

Geotechnical engineers engineer the ground that supports all conceivable man-made structures on the earth (land and water) visible to the naked eye, such as buildings, bridges, dams, railways, highways, rope-ways, industrial plants and mining plant infrastructure, towers, tunnels, silos, hill slopes in rock and soil, cable cars etc. A geotechnical engineer's role is to ensure a structure is provided with a competent (strong and stiff) foundation so that it stands safely through its design life period and does not sink (in soft, loose, marshy ground conditions), or falls (on hilly slopes), or slides or topples due to wind, water and/or earthquake loadings.

All structures, including off-shore structures, stand on the ground, which must be competent enough to support them. If the ground is not naturally competent, eg if it comprises a swamp or is inundated, it must be engineered to achieve its desired level of competency. That is where the geotechnical engineering professionals come in. They are responsible for keeping structures—building, towers, dams, bridges, roads—standing and prevent tunnels from collapsing.

The shape and size of structures, in view of their intended functionality—residential, public infrastructure and industrial—are conceived and designed by architects. Civil structural engineers undertake the necessary structural design to render a practical shape to that structure, whilst ensuring it serves its engineering purpose and does not collapse during its lifetime. It is the responsibility of geotechnical professionals to ensure the structure stands on the ground over its intended life, which is 50 to 100 years for most public structures.

Civil geotechnical and structural engineers ensure (a) a conceived structure is put into its intended shape; (b) safely stands proud on the ground with integrity; and (c) serves its intended function safely through its design life. Geotechnical engineering is a specialised branch of Civil Engineering that deals with the foundations of structures. 14th May is celebrated as the World Geotech Day.

Foundations! whether they are related to women's make-up, or the birth of institutions or countries, or primary education of the children, or the construction of buildings, bridges and towers, foundations are essential to support everything that is visible to the eye and stands on the ground. Foundations must remain hidden from the eye, forever buried, and keep supporting the structure. They don't have the luxury to come out and be on social media.

The word 'Geotech' refers to engineering and technology related to the earth—the ground—as the prefix 'geo' indicates. Geotechnical professionals—civil geotechnical engineers and engineering geologists—assess the ground strength and stiffness, and accordingly design and construct the foundations of structures.

The heavier and higher the structure, the heavier and deeper must be its foundation, which is analogous to humans who aspire to grow tall in terms of their stature in life.

Safe management of anticipated surface and ground water, and realistic imagination and consideration of long-term behaviours of soils and rocks sitting under the foundation of a structure, are amongst the most important aspects of geotechnical engineering. Note that soils and rocks degrade naturally with time, as do humans.

Due to the (unglamorous) nature of their work and heavy responsibility, with significant liabilities (as it is a matter of scores of lives who use a structure at one given time), geotechnical professionals are intrinsically shy and humble; their work remains buried in the ground so that the structures keep remaining standing and functional.

Overtime, as their work requires them to be deep thinkers, with a fair bit of imagination, many experienced geotechnical professionals develop into philosophers, accompanied with a distinct change in their general outlook and approach to life. Habitually, therefore, they tend to go deep into the root /source of problems for identifying possible solutions. It is for this reason that the author delves deep into the roots of various issues that the world and, in particular, India are currently facing—without getting distracted by the outward glamour of new shopping malls in India or the glamorous lifestyle of celebrities and neo-rich in India, both of which don't reflect the ground reality in the country.

There are striking parallels between geotechnical engineering and human behaviours and life, in general. Natural laws don't change! One reason could be that the human bodies, similar to the soils, are parts of the Mother Nature; both comprise a 3-phase system—solids, air and water. At the end of their journey, all humans go back to the soil where they come from. So, the laws related to the soils must also be similar to the laws affecting the humans. The four 'W's and one 'H' are the five essential steps for assessing the veracity of a matter—What, Why, When, Who and How. Scientists, engineers, doctors and lawyers are trained to use the process in their work. As children, being inquisitive, we all use these steps in our learning process but, as adults, some of us forget the process.

We—the so-called "educated" people—must not accept everything that is thrown our way, or spoken by anyone, whosoever he or she is, as a word of God. Individual dissemination, discrimination and discretion are necessary before we take any decision, or form any impression or draw any conclusion. Many people have suffered, and shall suffer, because of the way they were, or are being stereotypically portrayed by other people, either due to pure ignorance, or hearsay or deliberately.

The objective must be to foster mutual faith and trust between the members of this large global family so that everyone prospers and the real issues of diseases, poverty, education, environment and sustainability, corruption etc.—are nailed. Education is not literacy; education is much more than literacy. Education teaches civility and self-restraint. Education inculcates knowledge, patience, rationality in thoughts and wisdom. Wisdom and intelligence are two different things, with some overlap of course. Wisdom generally comes with age; there are reasons why army generals are grey haired.

> *Geotechnical engineers literally design, construct and maintain the foundations of civilised life.*

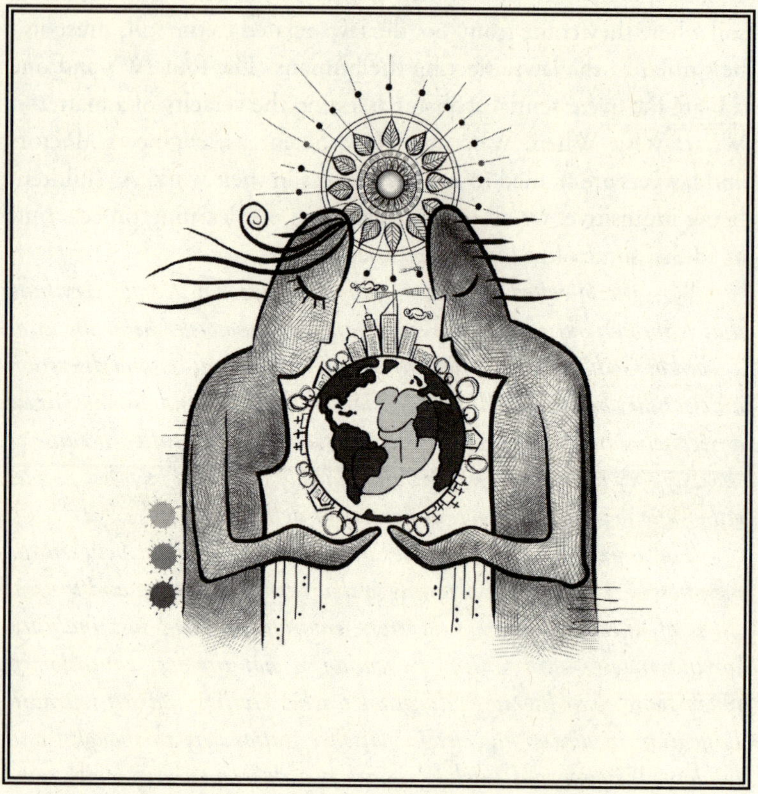

Be humble and grateful to the Mother Earth

Control the population for world sustainability

SEVEN

LIVEABILITY AND SUSTAINABILITY

Intelligent Fools on the Planet?

Wisdom may be the only gift that sets humans apart from machines, otherwise, in terms of intelligence, humans may soon become comparable and possibly find themselves as inferior to intelligent machines. Logically, the day may not be very far when humans find themselves in an awkward state of competition with machines that they are creating every day. The day Artificial Intelligence surges ahead of the average human intelligence, the human race may possibly start finding itself in a state of servitude and subservient to intelligent machines. The fact that machines are increasingly becoming more intelligent with time, thanks to the humans who have worked for the development and advancement of Artificial Intelligence, should put humans on notice that they may have unknowingly created a demon which may potentially devour them in the long run. The rise of Artificial Intelligence may possibly become a major reason for the ultimate downfall of the human race unless timely, adequate controls are put in place now to offset its long-term, irreversible detrimental effects.

Are Humans Making Themselves Redundant?

Humans invariably seek constant change, fun and excitement to distract themselves from a state of boredom that they tend to experience from their mundane, routine lives. They also constantly seek comfort and ease in undertaking their daily chores. In the past, they would use slaves but now they have created machines that are run by Artificial Intelligence. Their tendency to choose short-cuts in life, with least inputs, may be likened to a varying degree of escapism and malaise. Their imprudence may possibly erode away their core abilities to think, remember and enjoy simple pleasures of life. They are constantly replacing their traditional mundane tasks that have stood by them for the last 200,000 years of their existence, which they would generally carry out physically. For example:

- As pre-cooked food is available in the market, which just needs heating in a microwave or an oven, why cook food from the raw ingredients?
- As Google is supposed to know everything, why understand, learn and remember things?
- As GPS can provide directions on road, why bother to memorise the routes?
- If computer programmes can draw, design and calculate, why use hands to do them?
- If emails or text messages can be sent, why write?
- If design software apps can work, why should we undertake manual calculations?
- If robots and drones can work, why employ humans?

Simply, why bother doing anything if a machine can do it for you? Alarmingly, virtual sex is also known to have made inroads into some people's personal lives. As a major paradox, on the one end of spectrum, the underprivileged, who comprise the bulk of the world population, crave and work to make their lives comfortable with the facilities and gadgets that are mainly accessible to the minority, affluent population. On the other end of the spectrum, the affluent class may be making their own kind redundant by the mechanisation of their daily lives and over-reliance on gadgets.

Humans may, therefore, wittingly or unwittingly be making their own kind redundant and endangering the whole human race. One can see it happening in developed countries where versatile machines have started replacing humans in the construction, agriculture, health, transportation, sports and cooking industries. For example, remote-controlled, automated, driver-less trains and trucks have started replacing humans on large mining projects; on arrival—immigration process is done by machines with passports carrying micro-chips; and banking is done with automated teller machines.

Is Technology Breaking up Human Relationships?

On an individual level, addictive smart phones may seem to have brought the world closer—for example, through the use of social media etc.—it may have also created a greater physical distance between people. Social media, like any other facility available to humans, is seen to be increasingly abused and misused. On the negative side, it allows cowards to say anything—without taking any social, moral or ethical responsibility—and bully or malign anyone, which they would not otherwise dare to do in person. Families have begun to look like loose units that comprise individual members who may appear to live together but mostly choose to exist within the confines of their own virtual spaces. People choose to communicate through text messages and emoticons rather than express themselves in person.

Some people may argue if these gadgets and facilities are available and affordable, why should they not be used to make one's life easier. Yes, that is a valid argument but that may also gradually rob humans of their natural skills and independence. On surface, mechanised and robotic facilities may look attractive in making general life comfortable but, deep down, humans may be undermining their own very existence. "*We tend to lose what we don't use*", as the general principle goes and that applies to human faculties and skills. If we don't fully use our brains and memory, we are bound to become rusty, lethargic and incapacitated to think with time.

Undoubtedly, in general, as humans are fast relying on machines, they may also be losing many basic living skills in the process. Their reliance on machines may be deemed as acceptable on the proviso they do not render themselves handicapped in undertaking some essential chores of life—literacy, numeracy, cooking and breeding, and most importantly, the ability to think and philosophise, which qualify them as humans.

In essence, as long as humans are in control and machines work for them, the situation may be deemed to be acceptable. Objectively, what do we do with the time that we save by using the modern robotic facilities and electronic gadgets? Do we invest that time in our physical, mental, emotional and spiritual health? Are we happier than the times when these facilities did not exist? These are some of questions that we must ask ourselves now.

Going forward, humans must endeavour to wrest the core controls of their life back with themselves, and at any cost, not lose the ability to think, contemplate and philosophise to stay in control. The preservation of human feelings and emotional intelligence—with basic skills to innovate, acclimatise and survive—is necessary. Humankind needs to make serious commitment in education in arts—humanities, philosophy and literature to retain their thinking ability, emotions and feelings. Most importantly, children must be taught the skills of writing with hand, using paper and pencil or pen; solving mathematical sums using the traditional methods, without using a calculator; and doing basic cooking using raw ingredients. The arts of mental mathematics and calligraphy must be preserved at any cost.

Importance of learning and teaching literature and philosophy has never been as high in the history of humans as it is now. Humans must exercise both wisdom and intelligence to preserve their skills and race. Literature and philosophy are two of the best teachers for the human race.

Nature's Design to Control Human Population?

Despite the above argument, which has been made in favour of the need for the survival of the human race, some holistic thinkers and philosophers may also argue that Artificial Intelligence could be the solution that nature may have cleverly sought and devised (through humans only) for the survival of the planet that humans have been selfishly devouring. Does, therefore, nature intend to rescue the planet by gradually ridding it of humans who may have unwisely been growing their kind, which has been destroying and mindlessly devouring every natural resource on the planet? [Note that the human population has grown nearly seven times in the last 300 years and more than doubled in the last 70 years.]

Exciting times lie ahead, one way or the other as nature works both ways. We may have proved to be not only the most dangerous living species on the planet but also the most unwise species that has used its intelligence to undermine itself. We have created all kinds of weapons of mass destruction—nuclear, biological, and chemical—to destroy our own kind, through all kinds of warfare—cyber included.

> *Nature must be laughing at us fools. And, as the biggest living fools on the planet, we claim to be God's best creation and put ourselves at the top of the food-chain. Ha! There can't be any bigger self-deception, illusion and lie than that claim. Nature will have the last laugh, and it must. Nature is a great leveller. It gave us a chance to redeem ourselves but we may have squandered that chance forever—due to our greed and imprudence.*

Indian Population Growth is a Global Issue

The world leaders and all other world bodies members, such as UN, G8, G20, UNESCO, UNICEF, World Bank, Asian Development Bank etc. would do India and the rest of the world a great favour if they exert an unyielding pressure on India to urgently control its population or else be prepared for a number of human issues, including Super Bug epidemic, export of environmental refugees from India and a number of other serious human issues related to the health and overall well-being of Indians living in India. If China could successfully control its population growth, why cannot India follow China's lead and help itself?

India is one of the oldest and responsible members of the world community but does not exist in isolation. In this age of globalisation, India's problem is a world problem. The world community must put pressure on the Indian government to urgently introduce effective measures to rein in its unbridled population growth, failing which the fallout of India's population boom is going to adversely affect the whole world. India's population has grown fourfold since the British left the subcontinent in 1947. Currently, every fifth or sixth person in the world is an Indian. With a population of about 1.36 billion, India is currently the world's second populous country, but soon tipped to surge ahead of China as the world's most populous country. The election manifestos of major political parties in India have not historically included this existential issue.

The general fear amongst the Indian politicians and political parties is that if they speak about the need for population control, they may possibly lose the Muslim vote and the elections. Power corrupts and blinds the politicians to stark realities that sharply look them in their eyes. Like their Muslim counterparts, and most mainstream politicians, the Hindu religious leaders also don't exhort people to control their population; they fear India may have more Muslims than Hindus by 2050. So, this is a country where the two religious communities choose to suffer due to a continued environmental degradation rather than come together and defeat their common enemy.

Major businesses working in India from India and abroad—will not be happy with population control, as their market share will potentially reduce due to competition. Their mindset is driven by capitalism. The liveability of India, at least of its cities, is seriously impacted due to its high population. While the country is teeming with people, worsening air pollution and traffic woes characterise its cities.

a day. Many of them believe only nature may set things right in their country, as they seem to have lost faith in their country's vision. They foresee, and some desperately hope, natural disasters—earthquakes, floods, droughts, diseases—will reduce India's population and, thus, improve its ever-worsening living and environmental conditions. A 55-year old cab driver in Delhi even wishes a nuclear war breaks out and takes care of the population issue.

India cab drivers also struggle against a growing competition from other service providers. They blame the banks for enticing public with easy loans to buy cars. They also blame the government for not regulating the purchase of cars, as people, who have no car-parking facilities at their home, tend to buy more than one car and park them in the narrow streets outside their homes. [Note that the vehicle industry has been booming in India, as some 45,000 or more vehicles enter the countries roads every day, almost matching the net population increase each day (about 60,000)]. Cab drivers constantly move through the veins and arteries of a country—roads and streets, which depict the country's health—to be able to earn their livelihood. As such, their fingers are constantly on the pulse of their country. They are one of best sources of information about a country, company, organisation, family or an individual.

Wake Up, India

As history can testify, the greatest factors that have impeded the stability and growth of the Indian subcontinent, especially after the British left seven decades ago, have been its communal disharmony and distrust, cultural diversity and ethnic heterogeneity. On top of that, in India at least, the thriving caste system has been the icing on the cake. No sooner did the British leave the subcontinent than it divided itself into two countries. Another division followed 24 years later, in 1971. The border area between India and Pakistan is the world's heaviest militarised zone!

The subcontinent has indeed been fighting itself. The founding leaders claimed 'unity in diversity' as India's core strength. Only history will prove how far they were correct! India had to recreate a number of new states in the past decade or so. Creation of some more new states appears inevitable if one goes by the ongoing simmering power tussles and political undercurrents.

As proven by its neighbours, Pakistan and Bangladesh, even if, albeit in an unlikely scenario, all Indians converted and followed any one particular religion, her existential issues—a mindless high population growth, extreme disparity in the socio-economic structure, shamelessly naked and rampant corruption, disharmony and infighting amongst people from different castes and religious sects, and radicalising political polarisation—will continue unabated. The reason is that each religion has its own several sub-religious sects and their followers will keep fighting one another, as has been observed in India's neighbours, and the Middle East, where most people belong to one particular religion. In itself, therefore, religion may not be the prime reason for the woes of the subcontinent. But it certainly does provide the fodder and the base over which divisions are created, nurtured and exploited by power-mongers. Alarmingly, even the so-called educated people are seen to get polarised and blinded to facts. So, even education may not possibly help to erase social divisions.

Indians have a general cultural disposition to invent reasons to differentiate themselves from others—castes and sub-castes, religions and sub-religious sects, regions, languages, dialects and accents, food and, of course, the wealth. Even geological boundaries, such as rivers and hills, are used to create social divisions. The power-hungry polarising forces are proven experts in using religions and castes to create discord, disharmony and distrust between the people. The politicians continue to use the good old policy of '*divide and rule*' to grab and stay in power. They mirror the people whom they claim to represent. The past governments have also proactively fed and nurtured all social divisions.

Such countries, where social divisions are proactively nurtured and exploited by their political and religious leaders, can never become invincible or remain united for long unless and until the core reasons for social divisions and disharmony are nipped in the bud once and for all, and the lines of divisions are completely erased. But that is wishful thinking, at least in India, where even God may not succeed! The onus is on people and people alone, to cohere and harmonise. But will they? It is not unreasonable to expect that India, as a nation, will keep fighting itself till it achieves a logical equilibrium. Only one of the two possible results are inevitable, which any person of common sense can easily imagine. Despite that, God only knows which one result is actually destined for this country, where nearly one-fifth of the world population lives!

The World Order Keeps Changing

The world has changed significantly in the past seven decades. The leaders of the past have been replaced by the current new visionary leaders, who are expected to develop and follow relatively much more constructive and progressive policies than their predecessors.

The past baggage inhibits human growth and impedes national progress. What has happened in the past is dead and buried. Therefore, it is imprudent that buried bones be unnecessarily dug out. Why should one spoil the present with the past bitterness? Energies must be solely focussed on today, to heal all past wounds and then be able to surge ahead with greater zeal and enthusiasm.

> *Lord Tennyson said: The old order changes yielding place to the new and God fulfils himself in many ways lest one good custom should corrupt the world. Comfort thyself: what comfort is in me I have lived my life and that which I have done May he within himself make pure but thou If thou shouldst never see my face again Pray for my soul. More things are wrought by prayer than this world dreams of.*

Lord Tennyson's quote is so very pertinent to the current socio-political scenario in the world, including such a delicate relationship between India and Pakistan, their leaders and the people.

If Indonesia Can, Why Can't India?

Indonesian youth seem to be aware about the country's issues and are perhaps working consciously towards addressing them. They seem to be awake. A country belongs to its youth. When youth are awake, the country is awake. A young Indonesian academic, Ali Sabeni, has shared the following opinion about high population growth: "I can't believe that an engineer is talking about a country's issues … Honestly speaking, Indonesia has similar problems as India—population, education and unemployment, and the biggest problem right now is the religion. Our country has many religions and we live together without any problem. But at this point of time, as the presidential elections are to be held soon, some people create propaganda, using religion. And talking about education, although our university ranks at 300th position in the world, we are optimistic that it will improve in the future."

He added: "I have read your post; you teach me that we should care for our nation wherever we are. Population is our country's problem too. But Indonesia has started to take care of this issue. Our government has launched a campaign with a tagline *2 kids are better*. This campaign is active and visible everywhere—on the television, in newspapers etc. And I think it will have a positive impact … like my sister said, *let me have one kid, one but with a good quality*. If Indonesia can do it, why can't India?"

Are Young Indians Awake?

Are young Indians talking about their country's *population issue* in the public forum or on the social media? Are they awake like their Indonesian counterparts?

I am baffled when young people, who slog every day in ever-worsening traffic conditions in the capital cities of India and inhale polluted, poisonous air every day, advise me that I should not rant much about India's population issue solely because my readers may become bored reading the same old stuff. They advise that instead I should change the theme of my writings. It is extremely disappointing to see that such educated, grown-up Indians have virtually given up on any hope for improvement in the living conditions in their country. There is nothing more dangerous for any country than when its people simply give in without even putting up a decent fight. No wonder, the wealthy people and the influential politicians in India have either sent their children abroad to study and settle down there, or currently are in a planning phase to do so. Similarly, many young Indians too aspire to leave the country for greener pastures.

> *An unsustainable high population growth is the root cause of most of India's issues. Public discussion about population control in India is seemingly a taboo. No Indian television debate has historically touched this issue.*

Zero-Child Policy

"*No, Sir, India needs a Zero-child Policy*!" These words belong to a young frustrated couple on a motorbike, immediately behind our car, who, like us and hundreds of other commuters (mostly tourists), waited helplessly for that choked Dalhousie (Himachal Pradesh) road to open. They shouted these words immediately in response to "*India needs a One-child Policy*" that I had earlier uttered in frustration after stepping out of our car, having waited for more than half an hour, at a road-bend, for the traffic to move, with our engine running.

Many commuters—on two and four wheeled vehicles—looked visibly frustrated and helpless on that afternoon of 6 July 2018. A young female cop tried her best to facilitate the movement of traffic but there was a limit to what she could possibly do. Even though she was a policewoman, she could not widen the road or physically throw some vehicles off the road.

Hill Resorts too are Environmentally Vandalised

Dalhousie (named after Lord Dalhousie) has been a popular hill resort in Himachal Pradesh for more than a century. Like many other popular hill resorts, during summer holiday season, it suffers due to the invasion of humans from the nearby plains and chokes frequently. It has also contracted the diseases of cities—traffic jams, environmental pollution, frustration of commuters, mindless construction activity etc. The resort shows a clear carbon footprint due to an ever-growing human activity.

In July 2018, I visited Dalhousie after a gap of exactly 25 years, during which the resort seems to have become much denser, with many man-made structures featuring along the roads. The local roads have remained unchanged, as there is no possibility of widening them due to geographical, topographical and geological constraints. The roads have become more trafficked by pedestrians and vehicles—an obvious effect of increase in the number of tourists—due to climate change, unsustainable population boom and the economic growth of the country.

Kashmiris feel very uncomfortable in hot and humid conditions, as that is not their natural environment. Unfortunately, since their exodus from Kashmir, in 1990, they have suffered mentally and physically, during every Indian summer, and monsoons exacerbate their sufferings.

My father wanted a change and some quick relief from the hot and humid weather, so we decided to have a brief holiday at Dalhousie. We changed our hotel after getting caught in a severe traffic jam on the very first day of our arrival. From my last visit, I don't recall having observed traffic on '*garam sadak*' and '*thandi sadak*'. But now, these essentially pedestrian roads featured new hotel constructions and vehicular traffic.

Crippling traffic jams on those narrow hilly roads of Dalhousie, and similar hill resorts, not only waste precious human time but also damage the local environment. Dalhousie's local climate has seemingly changed.

Historically, Dalhousie would receive heavy snowfalls during winter months, in the order of four to six feet thick. Reportedly, however, last winter, it has received just two snowfalls, each only about six inches thick.

Possible Intervention Measures to Save Dalhousie

Dalhousie urgently calls for the following intervention measures to help save the local environment and the hotel industry itself:

- Introduce regulations to ban all new constructions in the area;
- During peak holiday season, carbon-emitting vehicles must not be allowed to move within a radius of about 5 km from Gandhi Chowk;
- Create a large car-parking facility at the downhill location, at least 5 km from Gandhi Chowk, where all tourist vehicles should be parked;
- Introduce battery-operated cars to transport the visitors from the car park to their hotels; and
- Introduce cycle rickshaws as local transport, which will provide employment to numerous people and also allow pedestrians to move safely and freely.

Tourists must be encouraged to walk around on foot. Ease in commuting is essential for maximising the benefits of any holiday or excursion.

What is the combined effect of population boom and the economic growth? Reduced liveability, increased mental stress and environmental degradation! What is the solution? Population and environmental control, as well as focus on making public transport more efficient and accessible, with strict control on the production, movement and ownership of private vehicles. Choked roads can be likened to choked blood vessels in a body, with potential catastrophic consequences.

Traffic jams on narrow roads in hill resorts are a sad result of a number of issues: Population growth, climate change, the new affluence of some, and mismanagement of the authorities and environmental irresponsibility of the local governments. Choking hills are the precursor to more difficult times looming in the future. As cities get choked and climate gets hotter, hills will be the next casualties.

> *One would only wish if Indians could think like the Chinese! If only the Indian leadership and stakeholders had the foresight, vision and the strength of the Chinese leadership and, more importantly, the will to address her population and pollution issues! If only winning elections and staying in power was not their single point agenda.*

Mother Earth

Mother Earth produces, nurtures, and finally accepts everything back. She refuses none. It does not matter how high you are flying, you will eventually come down to the earth, whether crashing or on your own device. She produces the aviation fuel that runs your aircraft, as well the materials that make your aircraft. Her love for all things that exist on the surface of the earth manifests through her gravitational pull. It does not matter how grand your house is or how high it is located above the ground, one day it will be demolished and everything that makes it will be returned to Mother Earth from where it came originally. It does not matter how much silk or fur or gold or jewels or diamonds adorn your earthly body now, one day your body and all your adornments and ornaments will also return to her. You are constantly nurtured by her—from your birth to your last breath. She provides you with everything that you need to survive and grow—your food, clothing, shelter, transport and everything else that you use or consume.

The animals that you feed on also feed on Mother Earth; they will also return to their origins—through you or directly. It does not matter how tall and strong you are, or how young and beautiful you currently are, your face and body will change before you return to her. Don't think too much about yourself, you are nothing but a speck of dust in the scheme of things! Live and be grateful for everything that you have received from Nature for as long as you are able to breathe, which is never under your control. Your each breath is a gift to you from Nature. With your last breath, all your pride, ego, knowledge and arrogance will escape with a puff.

> *Be humble and be grateful to Mother Earth. Bow to her, kneel down on the ground and kiss her. Remember, She gave you birth and She will take you back one day. You have nowhere to go but to Her. You will become a part of her one day.*

Human Rights & Population Control

'Can children be considered as humans?' If yes, do they have 'human rights' and, therefore, 'free will'? If yes, are they free to do anything they want? Do their parents and teachers allow them to exercise their 'free will', such as, play anytime they want; eat and drink anything they want; and watch TV for most of the time etc.?

Are children free to choose whether or not they want to study, go to school, wake up so early in the morning and carry that big 10 kg school bag on their back, sit for the examination etc.? The answer to most of these questions would be: "No, in the interest of their well-being—education, personal development, career, health, livelihood—parents and teachers cannot, and do not, allow children to exercise their 'free will' in respect to how they spend their time."In essence, therefore, it is the 'system'—parents, society, school, government, law&order etc.—that dictates what children 'must do' and, more importantly, what they cannot do.

As children grow into young adults, and then into adults, their behaviour and lifestyle continues to be dictated by the 'system'. There is no 'free will'! Because, in a civilised society, an individual's overall well-being (much beyond an individual's instincts and tendencies) and the society's greater interest dictate what an individual can and can't do. As an extrapolation on a much larger scale, if a country is suffocating and urgently warrants a strict control on her population growth, why should the pseudo-intellectuals construe population control as an infringement of human rights? Is an individual's human right—to keep producing children—higher than the basic survival and sustainability of the country itself? Isn't improvement in liveability, environmental sustainability and the survival of a country a common cause for one and all? Don't children have the basic right to grow and live in an environmentally healthy and habitable country, with access to abundant clean air and clean drinking water, security, authentic food and medicines, ease of movement on the roads etc.?

Let the policy-makers and leaders at the helm across the globe listen to the call of the time and act decisively in a timely manner—without falling into any strategic, political, social or religious bias—to control the world population before it is too late. Our earth does not have endless resources. The world, particularly the subcontinent, needs a range of out-of-box measures to contain its population issue before it consumes the planet and converts our beautiful blue planet into a living hell. Our planet has never seen so many people, so there is no previous experience or precedence of handling and containing the effects of this menace.

Due to a continued groundwater extraction, for domestic and agriculture use, and a widespread construction of heavy civil infrastructure—exacerbated by a significant population growth—Jakarta is currently sinking. Experts believe it may have just about 10 years or so to allow some stabilisation, if at all. Some portions of Jakarta are known to be sinking by as much as 250 mm/year. Some Indian cities may not be far behind before they too start showing geological distress. Who will bell the cat in India? The Indonesian government is considering moving their capital city to Kalimantan, but that will address only the symptoms of the disease, and not the core issue—growing human population and the construction of infrastructure.

A home defines its capacity in terms of the maximum number of people it can accommodate. So does an office, or a shop, or a school or a commercial centre. India must also define its maximum permissible population before its population becomes unmanageable. How often do we realise that we are just the temporary custodians of even the space that we occupy at this very moment—whether at home, office, and shops or on the road?

The space that we occupy now was occupied by some other people before us and will be filled by other people after us. If we don't own even the space that we occupy, we own nothing. This world was inhabited by entirely different people 100 years ago and will be

maximum density is reached in the soil at a particular water content, called Optimum Moisture Content, beyond which it loses its density, as water fills the pores between the soil particles instead of facilitating the compaction.

All materials follow a certain type of behaviour in their 'stress versus strain' relationship. Beyond a certain stress level, materials generally exhibit a plastic behaviour (means, they move towards an irreversible failure mode) and away from the initial (reversible) elastic behaviour. This law is applicable to human relationships also. For example, take the case of a rubber band. If you pull it beyond a certain strain level, its shape, size and strength will change irreversibly. Steel and soils also follow the same law.

In terms of human population, we may have reached, or are fast reaching a tipping point, and a human plague may be inevitable, as predicated by many philosophers and environmentalists. The pace at which humans are devouring natural resources and polluting our natural environment and habitat will undoubtedly come at an unimaginable cost.

Delhi is moving towards a lung cancer epidemic due to air pollution. Tuberculosis and cancer deaths are alarmingly high in the subcontinent, mainly due to environmental degradation caused by industrialisation and high population growth in the past half a century or so. The earth's climate is also changing fast. Let us hope prudence prevails. Hope humans wake up and use wisdom rather than emotions and conspiracy theories.

The land mass has the potential to sink in many regions of the earth as the groundwater table falls. Due to the ongoing global warming and climatic change, the seawater level will keep rising, which has the potential to inundate the lower-level coastal areas of many countries as well as many island nations. The greatest challenge before the current Indian leadership is to consciously improve the liveability in the country. If the environmental conditions are unhealthy and people are sick and unhappy, the country will never start on the path of progress.

The combined action of global warming and the loss of groundwater will undoubtedly exacerbate the potential loss of habitable land areas across the world. The groundwater must be allowed to recharge naturally and not be misused. India must urgently identify new sources of drinking water for human and animal use.

Our earth belongs to all of us. As its temporary custodians, we must look after it well and try to leave it in a better condition for its future custodians. Austerity, in consumption of natural resources is the need of the hour. Human population must be controlled worldwide.

India's Water Crisis

With a long shoreline bordering the peninsula, a rising seawater level due to climate change presents a serious challenge to India considering its large population, with an ever-increasing water and energy use. India derives about 80 percent of its water from below the ground surface. As such, the groundwater has been depleting fast due to a fast and growing human consumption and, alarmingly, may not last for more than 50 years from now. As a direct consequence, the land mass could also potentially start sinking. The overall consequences of a high groundwater use for the whole country are dire unless the population growth rate is fast stabilised in order to reduce the rate of overall consumption of all natural resources. Already some densely populated areas of India—such as Bengaluru and Chennai—are reeling due to less availability of drinking water. More areas will suffer in the future.

India is tipped to become hotter with time, which will exacerbate the increase in the consumption of energy, resulting in higher emissions and chest diseases.

Population Growth and Unhappiness

Power and wealth differentials are the main drivers for population growth and increase in human unhappiness. Advances in medical science and better healthcare have, of course, been the main catalysts for population growth. Religion too has been highjacked and misused for acquiring wealth and power. Human unhappiness increases as power and wealth differential widens. Man intrinsically strives for a full belly, pockets full of money and, finally, power and authority for the satisfaction of his ego.

Poverty is relative. Even the wealthiest keep striving for more wealth because they deeply fear their wealth may not be sufficient enough to keep them on that high social pedestal. They also fear someone else may rise higher than them or steal it from them. So they strive for more. They also remain psychologically insecure and surround themselves with bodyguards and security gadgets for personal protection. If there was no poverty in the world, no one would work for anyone. In such a case, it would not be easy for anyone to lord over other people, which is an egotistical necessity for the wealthy and powerful people. They all want to control others.

Our ego inflates when others bow to us, for whatever reasons. See how high we see ourselves when other people serve us at home, at restaurants and hotels, and in the wider service industry. Our ego controls and drives us. Relatively wealthier people need more people to serve them, massage their ego and lord over, and the relatively poorer people tend to produce more people to have more hands at work and to ensure their personal security. Absolutely rich people are rare; they just withdraw from the vicious materialistic cycle to ensure their independence.

> *Life was a dream and full of hope in the early eighties. Kashmir was a paradise. Delhi was green, with a blue sky, and looked exotic in the winter months. People were much more courteous, polite and disciplined. India's population was nearly half of what it is today.*

India's Liveability Issue

It is quite amazing why important matters, such as population and liveability issues, are not discussed in public debates in India. It is common sense that the energy consumption will keep increasing with increase in population, leading to poorer air quality, continued deforestation and worsening traffic conditions. Furthermore, a constantly growing inter-human competition will keep increasing corruption at all levels, adulteration, environmental degradation, and unhappiness, along with increase in mental anxiety and depression.

India does not have unlimited land mass, water resources and air cover, nor other natural resources. Unfortunately, it does not even has a vision like China, a country which controlled its population growth just in time and proudly emerged as a world leader and one of the very few superpowers. People are busy with matters of much lesser substance whilst the quality of elements that are necessary for human survival keep dwindling right in their face.

God and India's Liveability

Indian people and its leadership must carry out all that is necessary to help improve the environment and the liveability of their country. They can't leave it to God. They must attend to their mess themselves. God does not stand guard at India's borders—in 55 degree Celsius summer heat in Rajasthan and in minus 30 degrees Celsius in Siachin. God does not undertake surgeries in hospitals and grow food in the fields. If God has to do things for us, then why do we send kids to school? Why do we work? Why do we cook and eat? Why do we wash and bathe?

God is great and there is no doubt about it. But then why don't we leave everything to God and accept everything created by God, and sit back and relax? We don't, because we don't really believe that God will or should do everything for us that we are capable of doing ourselves. Nature has given us faculties. It is our duty towards God and Nature to make full use of our faculties and undertake all necessary endeavours to make this world a better place.

Without the human endeavour, we all would still be living in caves. God helps those who help themselves. No matter how much we pray to God for our individual wellbeing, wealth and success, our prayers have no meaning unless we look after our environment. Our greed will consume us. We dig our own grave by mindlessly producing humans who greedily consume the natural resources and poison the environment. God will not save us. God, why did you create our Mother Earth and us humans? You must surely be disappointed with us given how dangerous we are for our Mother Earth and all her life species.

What has our mother Earth gained by producing us? Not only are we constantly consuming her, we are acting against one another and other species too! One day she will gobble us up.Where people are constantly in a survival and competitive mode, they tend to be aggressive, just like other animals. In them, the feeling of real, unselfish love becomes non-existent.

My parents may have enjoyed a relatively good time in the sixties—and I in the late seventies and early eighties—but after that, it has been relatively darker and dirtier, and noisy. If humans are becoming sicker and unhappier, mainly due to an unhealthy environment, the economy loses its core meaning.

If liveability is dwindling with time, it does not matter how rich 'some' people are. If people and vehicles crawl on the roads and streets as mere ants, in growing smoke, with a grey sky overhead, breathing, drinking and eating poison—what is the economy for? Roads and streets act as veins and arteries of a country. If they are choked, it is imminent the country will anytime soon suffer from a paralytic stroke or a catastrophic heart failure. Indians will soon carry mini oxygen cylinders.

When CEOs comment on India's growth, they don't define 'growth'. Is it population, pollution, traffic, diseases, rapes, adulteration, road and pothole deaths, mental illness, happiness or student suicide? Or do they refer to the bank balance of the rich and the political elite? Unlike the Chinese, Indians have accepted liveability and sustainability issues. Strangely, Indians are preoccupied with useless, jingoistic political issues being discussed on mass electronic and social media. History will not forgive us for turning into ostriches. Our future generations will suffer immensely. They will curse us for our current impotence. That country will never progress in terms of liveability, honesty and happiness where education means literacy and rote learning, but does not encourage critical thinking.

I am a practical person—an engineer with a vision. I want to see positive results. I worry about the country and its present young and their future generations. I shall continue to ask questions. I don't want history to judge me harshly for remaining impotently silent.

Without a blueprint for the country, how do we know what we are trying to achieve, in how much time and through which processes and systems? These are simple and basic management requirements. Every corporation and company has a written vision for all stakeholders to behold, live and achieve. People must live the vision of their country.

As an engineer, it is unacceptable to me to run such a large and populated country as India, without a clearly defined vision. The country's Vision must be independent of the ruling party or the ruler. The ruling party, elected by the people in a democracy, is nothing but a contractor chosen by the people to deliver the country's vision, if defined, using proven and established systems and processes. It is the system that must run a country. India urgently needs to see VISION 2050 and VISION 2100 before it is too late. People must be given a glimpse of what India will look like for their children and future generations.

My Vision India 2050

Liveable India—blue sky, clean air and water, easy traffic
Educated India—100% citizens educated up to class 12
Safe India for women, children and elderly—no rape, no dowry
Sustainable India—population less than 1.5 billion
Healthy India—zero adulteration in food and medicines
Happy India—holistic education and spiritual way of life
Integrated India—one common Civil Law for all Indians

Democratic India—Presidential form of government with a two-party system

> *This is our time to do something. Let us sow positive seeds of hope, humanity and peace in the environment, through our ideas and writings. Let us play our role when it is still our time. One would hope there are people, who pick up these seeds and sow them far and wide, and then there are people who water those seeds, and then there are people who fertilise them and protect them from vultures, till we see a healthy and tall crop far and wide.*
>
> *Your true wealth is humans and the natural environment around you. Invest heavily in both.*

Height of Pride and Hollow Nationalism

India's problem lies with its people who chose to adopt an ostrich attitude and choose to turn a blind eye to her issues under the veil of false pride and hollow nationalism. Two years back, at the launch of my book, *Issues White-anting India*, two panel members in Bangalore, both bureaucrats, during a panel discussion, strongly reacted to my claim that India was becoming warmer and more polluted with time. One of them retorted, "India will be a nice, cool and pristine country in 2050 but, on the contrary, Perth (where I live) will be a polluted and hotter place at that time." Their reaction illustrated the reason why the country has been slipping in its liveability.

In India, many people react without thinking. How sad it is that a person who is desperately trying to raise the general public awareness about the issues that constantly undermine their country is being targeted and villified. All he wants is that you and your descendants live in a healthier, peaceful place. An iconic Kashmiri poetess of the past, Lal Ded, has said, "I saw a wise person starving to death and a foolish person beating his cook." She meant many (wise) people crave for learning from a teacher, whilst many (foolish) people beat their teacher.

It is unfortunate that people who enjoy immense power and authority and, therefore, ought to be awake and proactive in addressing existential issues in their country only demonstrate hollow nationalism and display a knee-jerk reaction, which reflects their vanity.

India's Population Woes

India has grown fourfold (from about 36 crore to about 137 crore) since 1947 when Indians were introduced to 'democracy' for the first time in their history. Unfortunately, they just could not handle and understand the core concept of democracy, simply because they were not familiar with it or even genetically predisposed to it. They love prostrating before power—money, authority etc. They love lording over other people and being lorded over.

As humans are also herd animals, their behaviour generally turns on its head—from settled and peaceful to more reactive and aggressive when they feel threatened—by competition or encroachment—when their number increases in a certain defined space. Like cats, their retractable claws come out. It has happened in India too. That is why many people think and act selfishly. People want quick benefits, without doing or sacrificing anything for their country. Being in a perpetual survival mode, due to everyday growing competition, they don't have much patience to wait and reap benefits in due course of time when good national policies and beneficial national schemes come to fruition.

The sustainable changes take time to occur, sometimes over a generation or two. Therefore, to bring about positive generational changes, an elected government must receive the mandate to serve the people for at least 25 years, i.e. one generation. As such, a 5-year period is just not long enough. Elections in India should be conducted after every 25 years, so that an elected government can focus only on nailing the issues and not find itself in an election mode within a couple of years after it is sworn in.

India urgently needs to implement a 'one child - one car per couple' policy to save its cities from further choking. If people ask for it, will any government implement it? If any government wants it, will the people accept it? Both scenarios look highly unlikely, at least at the present. There appears to be no awareness of the issue and a clear lack of vision and will on both sides.

Justice and Dignity stay together

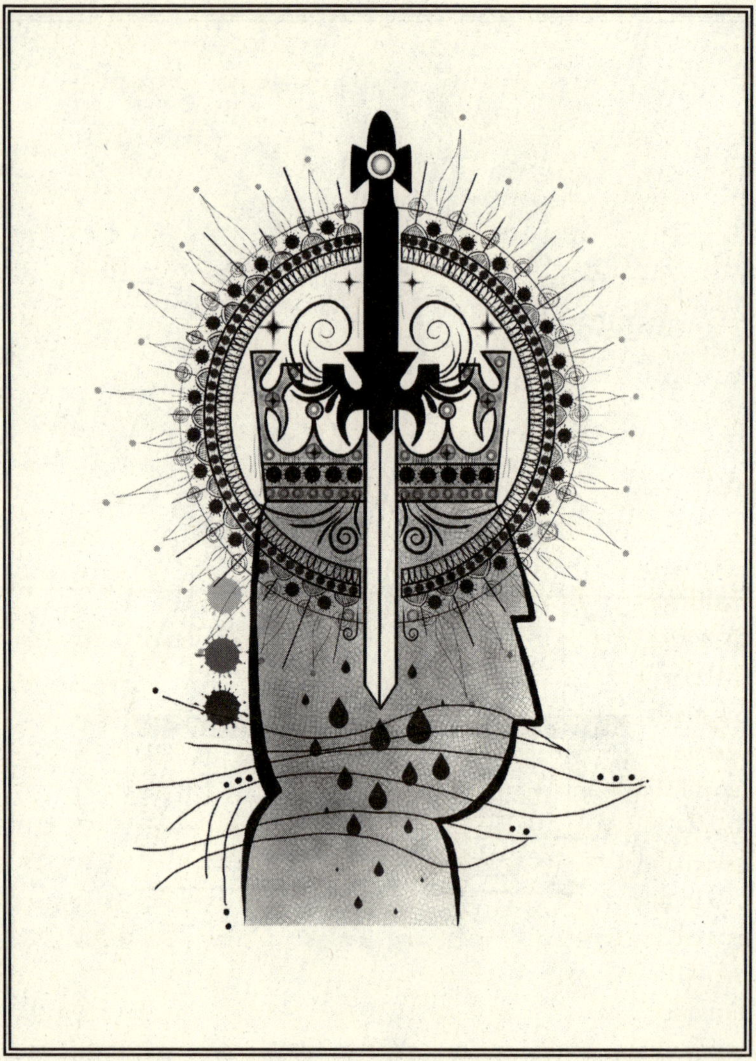

Power kills if it goes to head

EIGHT

POLITICS

Failings of Parliamentary Democracies

IN PARLIAMENTARY DEMOCRACIES, members of parliament (MPs) represent, or claim to represent, the voters within their respective constituencies. A political party that manages to secure more than 50 percent parliamentary seats, on its own or with the help of crutches provided by other political parties who ally themselves with the party, mainly to exercise immense political and administrative power that governance brings along, forms the government.

Ideally, all MPs of both the ruling party and the opposition are expected to carry equal weightage in the Parliament. But, practically, the MPs who belong to the ruling party enjoy disproportionate authority, power and influence in governance, which is understandable, as it is ultimately the government's neck that is on the line. An elected government is ultimately answerable to the people of the country; it is accountable for its failures in the same way as it receives accolades for its successes. In a majority government, the opposition practically becomes toothless and the ruling party, using all available parliamentary privileges provided by democracy and the Constitution, practically disregards the views of the opposition, whilst also endeavouring to muffle its voice in the Parliament. In a hypothetical scenario, if the ruling party has 51 percent of MPs in the Parliament and the opposition has the remaining 49 percent , half of the county practically remains unrepresented. The MPs who sit in the opposition fail to represent the people who may have voted for them.

In a flawed democracy, opposition is seen as an adversary and their opinions, views and apprehensions are generally overlooked. In essence, the government typically represents those people who vote for its MPs and not necessarily those people who vote for the MPs sitting in the opposition. The members of the opposition are, therefore, not able to deliver the promises made in the manifesto of its party, effectively leaving the voters in their constituency voiceless.

In a true democracy, the government is expected to make all reasonable endeavours to represent all voters—from both sides of the political divide. The government is expected to respect the mandate given by the voters to all MPs—in the government and the opposition—and, in doing so, listen to their views, apprehensions and all genuine, people-specific, human demands.

Some uncomfortable questions: How many governments can claim to uphold true democracies? For practical reasons—driven mainly by human bias and greed, corruption and the general human complexity—is it possible to achieve a true democracy that looks after all people of the country? Does the majority-vote system represent the core essence of a democracy? Is it ever possible that the ruling party and the opposition can work together as a team and look after their country?

India's General Elections

India, home to more than 1.37 billion people and claiming to be the world's largest democracy, with reportedly about 900 million eligible voters, recently celebrated its election festival, feverishly, with an unbelievable euphoria. None of the real issues undermining the country—population, pollution and education—figured in any of the election manifestos. In 2024, who will be held accountable—the people or the leaders? The amount of money reported to have been spent on election campaigns is mind-boggling. Who funded the campaigns? If only it was used for birth, crime, air and water pollution controls!

India is paying a heavy price for its political infrastructure and will definitely pay heavily in the future too. Its (ignorant) people—both educated and uneducated—are fully responsible for its condition. Politicians must not be blamed; they do what they always do. They make (unrealistic) promises to come into power and, thereafter, use semi-truths, unsubstantiated allegations against their opponents and distorted facts about the historical events and figures to mislead people and exploit their emotions for continuing to stay in power. Alarmingly and unashamedly, they also use raw muscle power and money—provided by hidden sources and faceless individuals—during those election campaigns to win votes.

India Needs a Constitutional Amendment

India claims to be a democracy but the country has not progressed, both in human and material terms, as much as China during a similar period of time. The reason is Indian democracy has been misused and not truly understood in its spirit. India needs an urgent constitutional amendment. Every government, including the Prime Minister—the Head of Government—must be appraised annually and three (3) months before the next general elections, by a team comprising the President (the Head of State) of the country, Chief Justice of India (CJI) and Chief Election Commissioner (CEC). During the appraisal, the overall performance of the government, in the light of the promises its members had made during the previous election campaign, must be critically reviewed. The appraisal report then must be made public before the next elections.

The appraisal process is logical because, at the time of inauguration of a government, the Prime Minister and his cohort of ministers take oath before the President. They must, therefore, be appraised by the President, who is the Head of the State of the union of India, in consultation with CJI, who looks after the legalities of the Constitution, and CEC, who monitors the election process and the veracity of the election promises. The appraisal process is similar to the appraisal processes used around the world by most private companies and government departments, where all employees are appraised annually for their performance over the year before decisions are taken by their employers about their continuation or discontinuation in the job, and their promotion or demotion, and salary increments or decrements, and bonus etc.

The government ministers are public servants, just like all other salaried government employees. They are employed by people and paid regular monthly salaries and perks, by tax payers, to do their designated jobs, and provided with necessary facilities, just like other employees. They must be paid half salary in the last three months before general elections because they spend most of their time in election campaigning. This constitutional amendment is vital for capturing the core essence of democracy in India and prevent a constitutional monarchy in the country. Governments must be held accountable for their performance and the promises they made to the people.

Ethnic differences, rather than religions, appear to be the main root cause of most, if not all social, political and military conflicts, at least in the last couple of centuries or so. This is exemplified by the two world wars in the 20th Century, Vietnam and Korean wars, Iran-Iraq war, Gulf war, and a bloody separation of East Pakistan (now Bangladesh) from West Pakistan (Pakistan) in 1971.

It is also reflected by perceived and proven differences between various countries in the Muslim world and a historical constant bickering between hundreds of Hindu princely states in the pre-Mughal and pre-British eras in the Indian subcontinent that finally led to the fall of the subcontinent to alien powers. It is inconceivable, therefore, in a hypothetical scenario, if Kashmir would have been happily married to Pakistan had it acceded to that country in 1947?

Kashmir is ethnically, culturally and historically completely different from both India and Pakistan.

> *In democracies, people are the boss and their elected representatives—Prime Minster, Ministers and the Members of Parliament—are in essence their servants. All government employees and bureaucrats are called 'public servants', as their salaries come mainly from the tax revenue paid by individual people and businesses.*

Kashmir

The central government in India must attend to Kashmir sincerely and pragmatically. Kashmir is home to about 10 million people. The Prime Minister of India must meet all Kashmiri people—in and outside the Kashmir valley—and also visit the Pandit refugee camps in Jammu and listen to their inhabitants. Kashmiris have long been suffering due to the insincerity and corruption of their leaders—both religious and political. The PM must listen to them.

Force is not the solution. Kashmiri hearts must be won for ushering in sustainable peace in the valley and speed up its development. Kashmir has seen the army since 1947. Sincere positive engagement with common Kashmiris is the first step to understand the issue. Not many Indian politicians have a clue about the issue, not to speak about the solution. There are more than 6 lakh homeless Kashmiri Pandits dispersed across India, many of whom crave for their home, especially when it becomes hot and humid in the plains of India. Genetically, they are not used to the hot Indian climate and its environmental conditions. Kashmiri hearts must be won, by sincerity and sincerity alone.

India—in terms of population, pollution, radicalisation and corruption—and Kashmir (in terms of unrest) are reaching a tipping point. Kashmiri Pandits remain an endangered community in exile, as political orphans. Strong decisions and decisive actions alone will define the fate of the country and the effectiveness of any government.

If the Kashmir issue is not resolved fast and Kashmiri Pandits are not home in the next 5 years, the current Indian government would have failed. Lip sympathy towards Kashmir and Kashmiris will not work anymore, as the world is watching. An unstable Kashmir and unsettled Kashmiris will not help the image and report-card of any government. The next 5 years are extremely significant for Kashmir and all Kashmiris. Kashmir poses a gigantic challenge for the government of India, which must prove its sincerity in winning the hearts of all Kashmiris—both the Muslims (in the valley) and the Pandits (in exile). For Pandits to return home, the valley must be first at peace.They are not cattle who can be transported and dumped within a secured barricaded area—like a concentration camp—in the valley, and alienated from their Muslim brethren.

Unless and until both communities live peacefully together, as neighbours, Kashmir can't be considered to be normal and at peace. Very hard testing times for all stakeholders lie ahead. How constructive it would be if leaders of political parties engage in positive debates only, i.e. highlight their successes and talk about their future plans to improve the lives of people. Negative politics and throwing mud at one another will hurt everyone in the long run. History teaches us a time always comes when we pay for our actions.

Kashmir is naturally gifted with minerals, oil, agriculture, tourism, artisans and handicrafts. Above all, it has intelligent young people. It has the potential to be an emerging resource and service economy, like Australia and Singapore, in addition to being a world-class tourism destination like Switzerland. My dream is to convert Kashmir into a regional hub of world-class education, a regional convention centre, buzzing IT services' centre, and a summer and winter sports destination. I want to see Kashmir roar as a majestic lion, progress with confidence and live the glory of its distant past as a shining economy.

In a polarised community, a centrist takes the heat from both poles. The leftists see him as a rightist and the rightists see him as a leftist. It is, therefore, much easier to shout from the extremes but very difficult to stay calm in the centre; one needs to be brave, with strong convictions.

The call of the hour is to stitch all communities together. People's mutual confidence and trust is paramount, as a foundation for sustainable stability, peace and progress of a multiracial and multiethnic country. All people must feel included and looked after. The political leadership must represent each and every one. Kashmiri Pandits could have been a key asset and an essential part of the solution, in 1989-1990, but only if they had been taken into confidence by their Kashmiri family members. They are still a big part of the solution. Unfortunately, they became a collateral casualty and fell through the cracks. They continue to be political orphans. One entire generation of Kashmiris—Pandits and Muslims—disappeared into oblivion in the last thirty years whilst craving for peace and return of Pandits.

Kashmiri Pandits left Kashmir for a reason. Thirty years later, the same reasons seem to prevent them from returning. Where has the government been these past three decades? How many decades more will the government take to wake up? Planes crashes, due to pilot errors, bad weather or mechanical failures, but humans do not stop flying, unless systemic issues occur with planes or the airlines. The return of Kashmiri Pandits to Kashmir is figuratively similar to air travel—a leap of faith, without guarantees. Kashmiri Pandits can return to their homeland only when their Kashmiri Muslim brethren accept them back wholeheartedly. No politician or political party is honest and capable enough to bring about that 'magical' acceptance.

Force can never bring hearts closer, even if the entire world's armies were to combine and comprise such a force. Kashmiris must be won by love and care and not force. Kashmiri Pandits are constantly being used, misused, abused and deceived by hollow claims and false promises of politicians. They must individually reconnect with their Muslim brethren, same way as they had left Kashmir individually, without allowing any fake involvement of any politician, whosoever he or she may be. "A closed mouth catches no fly," so goes an old English saying. Kashmiri Pandits may continue to be called Kashmiri migrants for next three decades or so and then will certainly be forgotten, especially after their current middle-aged generation passes on. Tragedy is not many Kashmiri Pandits will be left to celebrate Haerath Day after 2050 in the traditional Kashmiri manner and fervour.

Pandits are left with just under 30 years or so to revive themselves as a community. It is essential they return to their mother valley—their Maej Kasheer—before it is too late. For that, it is paramount Maej Kasheer attains peace and, more importantly, their Kashmiri Muslim brethren extend a helping hand to them. Only when Maej Kasheer is complete with all her children and, therefore, happy, all Kashmiris will benefit with her rich blessings. When your (blind) loyalty is taken for granted and you become predictable, you start getting marginalised and taken for a ride. You are considered as a "low maintenance" commodity. Your leaders feel assured of your (unwavering) support. They don't feel any need to give you much in return. No wonder some vulnerable and endangered communities, such as the Kashmiri Pandits, hardly get their fair share of treatment and benefits from their government and political leaders.

I have a dream, a dream of an educated, prosperous and vibrant Kashmir, where both communities cohere peacefully and thrive amicably, bring their respective best to the table and exemplify a great community.

I have a dream of a modern skyline of a new, clean Kashmir; of a Kashmir which is the regional hub of world-class education and a regional convention centre, as it was in the past when it was called Sharada Peeth; of a Kashmir which is a regional business hub and service industry, as Singapore is; of a Kashmir which is a regional hub of summer and winter sports; of a Kashmir which is a world class tourist destination, as Switzerland is; of a Kashmir which is a vibrant hub of culture and spirituality, where temple bells and aazaan from mosques together produce a beautiful spiritual melody, as in the past; of a Kashmir where Id and Haerath are celebrated by all Kashmiris with great traditional fervour.

Come, join me and see this dream realised. Let us work together to translate this vision into reality. We Kashmiris must work together to reweave our unique *Koshur* fabric of *Kashmiriyat*. Let us all put our best foot forward, throw away the baggage of the past, and look forward to a vibrant peacful Kashmir.

A Wish for Kashmir

- A peaceful, progressive and prosperous Kashmir.
- Kashmiri Pandits willingly and peacefully living—as prominent citizens—in the valley of Kashmir with their Kashmiri Muslim brethren.
- India and Pakistan joining hands and together fighting their common enemies (terrorism, poverty, poor education, gender discrimination, disease and health issues) like two mutually trusting and friendly blood brothers.
- Professionals from India and Pakistan (teachers, engineers, doctors, artists, journalists, academics and others)—from all religious backgrounds—working in each other's countries, similar to Aussies and Kiwis.

Hinduism

Hinduism (Sanatan Dharma) is not under any kind of threat; it never has been or will be, as long as it is lived as a philosophy, and not as a religion. We must stop this 'divisive' fear campaign. The terms Sanatan Dharma mean eternal faith. Can oceans be threatened by rivers? All rivers flow to meet the oceans. Oceans are the reason for life , for the formation of clouds, rain and snow, which feed the rivers. Oceans feed the rivers which merge back into it, as humans merge back into earth. Hinduism, in its original philosophical form, is like an ocean—-vast, deep, free, flexible, all inclusive, all embracing, and all giving!

Let us not give Hinduism the rigidity or boundaries of a religion; it will overflow all boundaries. Let us not make it a religion. Let us not make it rigid. Rigidity is weakness. Rigid things break. What threatens Hinduism? Who has threatened Hinduism? Is Hinduism decaying that it needs to be revived? What is Hinduism? These are some questions which must be answered honestly to address a general (wrong) perception driven (by fear) in modern India.

Most people who are made to believe Hinduism needs revival may not even be aware of the fact that Hinduism is a philosophy—a way of living—but NOT a religion. The word 'Hindu' does not even figure in the original Hindu literature—*Shruti, Smriti* and *Puranas.* People must understand the lessons from the Ramayana and the Mahabharata. They are not mere stories, they are philosophies in action. They are deep and profound. There is no better practical guide to living life than the Bhagwad Gita. Understand and live the Hindu philosophy.

Lessons from the Mahabharata

Vidhur (from the Mahabharata) left the Kaurava camp after being continuously frustrated and repeatedly jeered and scoffed at by the Kauravas. He was called *Soot-putra* (son of a maid). Vidhur was a wise person, with an open mind. He saw wrong things happening in the Kaurava camp and singlehandedly kept resisting the wrong behaviour and unfair and unjust actions and thoughts of Duryodhana who, in his gigantic pride and arrogance, would not listen to anyone other than a group of sycophants. So many great personalities either chose to turn a blind eye to his wrongdoings or lacked the courage to oppose him for fear of the consequences of opposing him. Vidhur was the most wise and righteous of all Kauravas. He repeatedly faced and opposed an arrogant Duryodhana, without fear or bias, and told him that his actions were unjust, immoral and unfair. Vidhur left the Kauravas and survived. Vidhur was the only real friend of the Kauravas—other than Krishna. He tried his best to instil wisdom in the Kaurava clan, till he left them in disgust. He had the guts and selfless wisdom to oppose arrogant Duryodhana. All other wise and brave people, who kept slavishly quiet, and other foolish sycophants perished in the Mahabharata war. In the Ramayana, Vibhishana was another such person.

Duryodhana was very brave and mighty but he lacked the noble vision, due to his intoxication with lust and power. Lord Krishna repeatedly tried to advise him and restore some sanity in him, albeit for his own wellbeing—-as the Lord intended to be fair to both Kauravas and Pandavas—but Duryodhana kept ignoring his wise counsel. Lord Krishna even gave him the first choice of choosing between Him (Lord Krishna) and His army in the looming war of the Mahabharata. But in his arrogant, unwise, vision-less state of mind, he opted for Lord Krishna's army instead of the Lord Himself.

Lord Krishna ended up being on the Pandavas side, but decided to be the great Arjuna's charioteer only (and not fight)—once again choosing to be impartial. The five Pandava brothers won the war, simply because they continued to fight for the *dharma* (morality, fairness justice and righteousness). Most importantly, they had complete faith in the Lord and themselves. They acted and fought to their maximum individual abilities, without leaving all their duties to the Lord. They did not say Krishna would do everything for them. They did what they were born to do.

One must never leave the path of righteousness, despite undergoing immense sufferings (as the five Pandava brothers did), as the Great Almighty will carry you when it matters the most. It is also important to add—-as the Mahabharata teaches—-that wars don't leave anyone anything to be proud of. Although the Pandavas won against a much bigger and formidable opponent, they had nothing to rule over, as not much was left. So much was destroyed and so many humans died.

Lord Krishna has taught that reconciliation is the best approach to resolve bitter issues, as the consequences of war, even if a 'dharma yudh', is unimaginable and unacceptable. Both parties lose, practically. Therefore, it is important that prudence, fairness, justice and wisdom are allowed to work out their noble magic during negotiations and resolve the issues peacefully. Then both sides win.

Capitalism and Communism

Should those humans who are wealthy, clever and powerful consume those who are not as wealthy or as smart or powerful? Does power and intelligence make a real difference between the 'consumer' and the 'consumed'? Well, that happens in a capitalistic world. If you don't consume, you will be consumed. The capitalistic world is all about the survival of the fittest. Sink or swim!

> *Capitalism creates socio-economic classes and social divisions. On the other hand, communism does not recognise or promote the individual human endeavour. Both are unsuitable for human happiness. There is a middle ground somewhere between the two where we humans need to stand.*

Politics in Social Media

Like politics, social media is not for the thin-skinned or the faint--hearted. In this day and age, as a lethal weapon, it can potentially destroy individual people, families, communities, organisations and even change the fate and course of countries. You must be in control of your time and activity on the social media. If not, social media has the potential to control you and ruin you completely.

Four types of people remain active on the social media:

- **Tigers**: Being natural leaders, they propose their independent thoughts and perceptions, philosophy, and suggestions about social engineering etc. They comprise up to about 5 percent of the users.
- **Self-Worshippers:** They comprise up to about 50 percent of the users. Generally, they post their selfies and pictures taken at social events. They love advertising themselves—their social activities, personal and family achievements, social contacts etc.
- **Cattle:** They form about 40 percent of the users. They act as posties or delivery people. They receive and forward the posts of others. Sometimes, they also stamp the ideas of

others by using emoticons. They are used and exploited by politicians and religious leaders to spread and promote their ideologies and the agenda.

- **Vultures:** They are sadistic *grave diggers* and form up to about 5 percent of the users. They have nothing of their own, as they are not creative enough. They are the ones one must be extremely wary of.

The *vultures* are the major cause of grief and destruction for many unsuspecting social media users. Being generally sadistic, vultures derive immense pleasure in sinking others. Generally, they try to target and malign the lions, sometimes even the cattle, especially if they don't like them for personal or any other reasons. They sneak in quietly and remain hidden. They never reveal their true self, they just watch quietly. As soon as they find a vulnerable post, or mistake their target's post as potentially contentious or controversial, they pounce in to get their prey. On many occasions, however, they lose their feathers, claws or even their beak, only because of their miscalculation and misreading their target.

The members of the first three groups must always identify the vultures, if possible, right in the beginning and then remain always wary. Note that most of them are like chameleons. One of the best ways to deal with the vultures is cold treatment. Just ignore them and never accept their hawkish challenges. Never fall to the temptation to respond to them, howsoever, tempting it may be. As vultures are not very wise or creative enough, their attack does not last long. They derive their strength from the reaction of their target. If you don't react, they will implode silently.

Be alert, be smart. Don't react when someone tries to be aggressive. Ignore that person. You may be clever enough to turn the tables and defeat that person, but think wisely and don't react. Are you on social media for the right reasons or just to feed on others?

Please engage only in civil conversations. Do not make anything personal. Follow ethics strictly. Human beings have intrinsic dignity, so uphold that dignity. Just withdraw if the other person is getting nasty. Do not get involved in unpleasant exchanges however much someone tries to provoke you.

> *A user (rather abuser) of the social media, in particular, one who is not in control of one's activity, has the potential to suffer from Obsessive Compulsive Disorder (OCD) and paranoia, leading to unnecessary waste of human resources and precious time, and even life. In addition, if bullied by one's so called 'friends', one can suffer from severe mental anxiety and depression disorder. Many people, both young and adult, do become victims of bullies; unfortunately, many are driven to commit suicide.*

A Country is as Good as its People

People make and shape a country. A country is defined by the values, conscientiousness, citizenship and discipline exhibited by its people. Politicians are just the sample representatives of the people. Unless people improve qualitatively and conscientiously, the quality of politics and politicians will never improve. Politicians alone must not be blamed for those issues. They are born out of people, so people must accept their equal share of the blame too.

You may receive a blank look when you ask a common person: "What are you prepared to do and sacrifice for the country?" In some cases, they may react: "What can we do, we work hard to survive? We pay tax. The corrupted system will not allow us do anything. Nothing will happen unless we have good leaders." People carry immense expectations from their governments and leaders but, strangely, do not spell any expectations from themselves. They don't realise their leaders and lawmakers mirror their own reflections. Undoubtedly, the country needs good politicians but that will not happen unless the country produces good citizens. People will keep getting what they deserve.

The tragedy is that educated and wise people, who can make such a significant difference, are happily and silently watching their country drifting along. Some even defend the system! One must imagine Sisyphus happy! Paradoxically, but not surprisingly, most of them strive to send their children abroad, for education and permanent settlement. Perhaps, they know the state of future living conditions in the country.

Indian People Must Wake Up

Whilst India's brightest minds work at the cutting edge of science and technology, its policy makers and politicians endeavour to divide the country along the regional, religious, ethnic and caste lines. For a reason, religion and caste, and not the human well-being and development, drive and characterise the Indian political thought. Indian politicians have polarised the Indian community.

The country pays a heavy price for its uncontrolled population growth and the accumulation of wealth by a small minority, whilst it also witnesses a steady erosion of its traditional civil, social, environmental and moral ethics. The county's current value system is characterised by the people's poor uncivil behaviour on the roads and general lifestyle. People play loud music during the night hours at social and religious events, without a care for any sick person or a student in the neighbourhood who may be preparing for examinations.

Different sections of the Indian community live in different ages, and pull the nation in different directions. Unless they all move together—coherently—into the current day and age, India will keep paying heavily for its people's faults. Who can bring people together to achieve the common goals of country's health, sustainability and prosperity? Only people can, they are the *People Power*. But that will happen when they wake up, when they are educated, when they become determined to bring about a generational change. To give vent to their frustration, out of sheer desperation and a short-term memory loss, people exercise their democratic right to vote, which allows them to keep changing the governments, but only to find themselves back in the same old situation. Their impatience, lack of vision and lack of character work against them in the broader terms and damage the country as a whole in the longer term. Change is the only constant in India, and not the human development.

Myopically, due to lack of a national character, most Indians don't care what happens to their country in five years or 100 years. They just want quick fixes so that their daily lives improve dramatically without any input from them. No wonder they fall prey to irresponsible election promises (equivalent to bribes), such as reduction in electricity bill or waiving off farming loans, not even questioning once how any government can afford such luxury overheads.

The common people struggle in their daily lives regardless of who lords over them. Many of them—especially those who produce more than two children (some up to six or more from one wife, or many more children from several wives)—must be blamed for their poverty, illiteracy and daily struggles.

If people don't work and care for the country, and put their country before their own self, they must not expect their leaders to do any magic for the country. Only when people realise enough is enough, let us rise and help ourselves, magic will happen! Unless and until that happens, India has absolutely no hope.

India follows a Westminster form of governance, not a military dictatorship. People have the democratic power to vote. If people don't exercise their sacred right to vote judiciously, with prudence and vision, they must not expect India to improve dramatically. Indians must choose their representatives carefully, solely based on merit and past performance, and not just emotions. The onus is well and truly on the people of India. The People Power matters in a democracy otherwise bring in a benevolent dictator to run and manage the country.

Survival of the Fittest in India

Survival of the fittest proves humans are like other herd animals. If you don't wield political or money power and look physically strong and threatening, you will be consumed by others, one way or the other.

Your body language changes as you become wealthy—your gait, language and tone, and your handshake. You will be expected to know and brush shoulders with the important and influential people—in government and political circles, business and media circles, and the police and judiciary. Most importantly, you will be known and feared for your sting; therefore, people will speak to you with utmost respect and subservience, albeit what they will call you behind your back is another matter. For earning respect in India, one does not need academic degrees or knowledge. Money talks in India if you are able to wear expensive designer clothes, heavy gold jewellery and diamond rings, drive expensive cars and live in expensive areas and in large houses. With lean-looking, poorly-fed, servants buzzing around you, you tend to think you are no less than a god. In India, power and money are worshipped.

Corruption in India

As a direct result of mind-boggling population growth and an ever-growing competition—driven by ever-increasing *demand to supply ratio* in most walks of everyday life—corruption has become an accepted way of life in India, so have bullying, aggression and arrogance.

People have developed very ingenious ways of individual survival and prosperity, most of which pass through the paths of *corruption*. Ironically, many see corruption as a normal way of life—*aisa he hota hai, sab chalta hai, mainu kee, kya problem hai?* For individual survival, most people watch mainly their own individual interests.

A prevalent herd mentality and mental blindness—to feed mindless social extravaganzas—have given birth and acceptability to corruption. The lavish lifestyle of the rich and the famous drives corruption at all socio-economic levels, because the common person wants to mirror them.

Not many people are capable of even thinking for a moment what they are doing and what they ought to be doing. Peer pressure and tendency to show off amongst the middle-class makes them blindly follow the everyday social trends set by others, such as novelties in lavish weddings, private schooling, expensive holidays and outdated rituals etc. A relatively honest person, who falls to social pressures, ends up becoming poorer. Brave and conscientious people, who exercise austerity and don't indulge in corruption or social extravaganzas, risk being called black sheep and outcasts. An average person who does not have money for bribing officials generally suffers.

> *In an ethnically, socially and economically heterogeneous India, it is not possible to make all people happy unless they are educated and made to work conscientiously for the country, and demonstrate a national character.*

Major Challenges before Indian Leaders

- Address the main issues plaguing the country, such as population, liveability, education, corruption, security and rapes, poverty, dowry and lavish weddings.
- Get rid of divisive politics driven by religion, region and caste.
- Represent 'all' Indians, regardless of who they are, and remain blind to religious, caste, gender and socio-economic backgrounds of the people.
- Be immune to (corruptible) influence of the wealthy and the influential in the country.
- Introduce a *uniform civil code* in the country i.e. one law for 'all' Indians.
- Put full brakes on India's population growth, using all available just and humane methods—education, print and electronic media and a vigorous social campaign—through all necessary bureaucratic, legislative, administrative and legal procedures.
- Rebuild and repair, as necessary, India's educational infrastructure—with double spending on education across the country (to at least 8-percent of GDP).
- Make school education free and compulsory for 'all' children up to Class 10, with implementation of punitive measures for defaulters.
- Enforce teacher appointment based solely on merit, with

compulsory continuous professional development and the accountability of teachers.

- Make primary and pre-primary school education 'holistic', without any written assessments, and facilitated by the best minds (teachers) from the country, who should be remunerated at the highest levels, and rewarded with all necessary perks, allowances and incentives to work in every nook and corner of the country—of course, with full accountability and penalty for defaulters.
- Eradicate rape from the country. Rape is the most heinous crime against women, who comprise half the humanity. The law must instil deep fear in potential rapists to achieve full deterrence. To nip it in the bud, exemplary punitive measures should be introduced in letter and spirit so that no male will ever dare to even think about committing this crime.
- Make dowry—both offering and accepting—completely unlawful and a serious crime, with 10 years of rigorous imprisonment to both parties.
- Regulate wedding expenses to control corruption.
- Put a strict control on the purchase of motor vehicles—in terms of both their size and the total number per household. Motor vehicles must not be allowed to be parked in single-lane streets. People must not be able to own a motor vehicle unless they have a parking space within the boundary of their property.
- Introduce a law under which food and drug adulterers are served with nothing less than death sentence, to ensure complete deterrence of the crime.
- Sharpen enforcement to nip corruption in the bud. Enforcers should also be closely monitored to make sure they are honestly doing the job for which they are paid.

Indian Weddings Fuel Corruption

Lavish weddings and dowry need exorbitant amounts of money, which a common person is not able to afford from one's normal

and external—who feed on the current social and religious divisions and exploit them by using the proven age-old 'divide & rule' policy for their selfish and evil designs. In the absence of such a powerful unified fist, not only will the hand certainly fall off but the whole body may potentially disintegrate.

It is high time all socio-religious leaders join hands and work together to put this confused country on the path of sustainable peace and progress, and ensure its environmental sustainability. They all face the same living and liveability issues every day. They all have the same common threats and enemies. Their historical coexistence has proved that they are not enemies of one another. However, their common enemies have successfully confused, misled, divided and exploited them deliberately and made them to be fearful and apprehensive of one another.

Pray India wakes up! Focus on the people in the middle, who comprise the bulk (about 80 percent) of the humanity. Remember the 'bell' curve (Gaussian or Normal Distribution Curve). People with extreme views swing from one extreme, like a pendulum, to the other extreme. People on the fringes will remain there till they don't consciously move towards the core. It is a sheer waste of time to focus on a fool or a genius. A fool won't understand you and a genius does not need you at all.

The next five years will prove the vision, honesty, strength and sincerity; or, alternatively, the incompetence, impotence and ineffectiveness of any government in India. The next five years are the acid-test times for the people and their leaders. In all probability, based on the past performances of all governments since 1985, one can't expect any miracle to happen in regard to population control and the hopeless cause of Kashmiri Pandits in the next 5 years. If the current Indian government proves to be as ineffective as earlier governments, India will continue to limp on.

The onus is well and truly on people like us. We must try our level best to bring about this important change in the country. Politicians are answerable to people and they must listen to people.

We owe our sincere, sustained, selfless efforts to our current younger generation and to their children. History may never forgive us if we choose to keep quiet, or pretend to be blind and deaf, and fail in our efforts. Can the current Indian government rise to the current challenges facing the country and prove its worth?

Indian Television must Debate Population Issues

Has there ever been, or will there ever be, a public debate—on the television or in the published media—about the maximum population that India, as one nation, can afford to have? For TRP reasons, one would expect no private television channel in India ever touching this issue in the country. The government run, Indian television channel *Doordarshan* claims to be different from most private channels in terms of its core objectives, social engineering, education and service to the nation. Therefore, should *Doordarshan* not rake up the population issue, as its service to the nation, and its accountability to the current and future generations, before it is too late?

History may Never Forgive Us

I apologise to those readers who may get offended by my writings and thoughts. All I intend to do is to draw attention to many serious issues faced by India. I wish you to join me in raising our unanimous voices that reach the relevant stakeholders, and Indian government, so that those issues are addressed effectively and the country thrives.

Instead of focussing on political leaders, and comparing their strengths and weaknesses, why can't we focus on the country? Instead of negative campaigns against any one of them, let us endeavour to undertake positive actions for the country. Follow your leaders and act consciously for the benefit of your country, instead of indulging in people-worship or any idle gossip. Actions alone matter. Let us all show active citizenship and love for India through our actions, and actions alone.

People make the country and our positive actions alone will help to save it and make it a better place. By our casual indulgence in social and political gossip, through the misuse of electronic mass media or social media, all of us are just wasting our precious time and the human resources. In doing so, all of us cause further damage to the country, some due to sheer ignorance, some due to indifference and some due to inaction. Instead, we could all pool our resources and act together to save the country. How nice it would be if political leaders transcend their personal ambitions and party gains, and instead work with one other, as one team, and earnestly address the issues facing the nation.

> *Bhakti must be shown towards the country. It is similar to religion. If you worship Lord Ram, let your personal character and actions mirror Lord Ram's, as a mark of your worship. Similarly, if you worship Lord Krishna, then follow his instructions: act decisively (without expectations) and don't witness wrong things happening passively. Worshiping your deity or your favourite leaders, for your personal materialistic benefits, is of no use to anyone—to you or the country.*

People Waste Their Time with Conspiracy Theories

Sometime around the end of 2018, the Indian television and social media was abuzz with rumours of a suspected assassination plot against a high profile leader in India. The extent of madness was such that the suspected plot was being fervently debated on Indian television channels, as if there were no other existential issues in India that should have been debated?

A friend in India seemed overly concerned about the suspected 'assassination plot'. My father also seemed worried. I assured both that nothing untoward would happen to their beloved leader; it was only a deliberate rumour to cause public panic and possibly generate a sympathy wave. Based on common sense, if somebody would have really wanted to do something like this, why would it be broadcast and discussed? Such clandestine operations are undertaken with utmost secrecy for maximising success. If Indian intelligence and security had got a sniff of any assassination plot, why did they leak it? Such rumours generate social gossip, hike TRP of television channels and generate a sympathy wave. Note that the 2019 general elections were approaching.

Logically, it seemed quite unlikely that any foreign hand could have been behind any plot. But Indian politics is ridden with negativity. People-based and party-based politics keep people engaged in their homes, at social gatherings and over social media. Fear-psychosis is used to tailor people's opinions and voting preferences. Social media has undoubtedly taken a great toll on the common sense of people, even of the so-called educated ones, through those crafty doctored videos and false stories that show the political adversaries and political opponents in poor light. Public fails to realise that assassinations don't follow television debates or propaganda or any kind of advertisement. Common sense says such plots remain shrouded in extreme secrecy till they are carried out successfully; and, thereafter, many cases remain unsolved mysteries for years. But, these days, common sense is not so common in India because it has been replaced by the social media.

Indian history is full of examples of insider jobs, treason and treachery. Mahatma Gandhi, Indira Gandhi and Rajiv Gandhi were all assassinated. Politicians of this day and age are not stupid people; they know any such misadventure will potentially backfire and will literally burn the country—causing widespread anarchy—and no one will benefit. Indian politicians may be cunning and selfish, but not so stupid that they will 'kill the goose that lays the golden eggs'. A democratic country where salaried politicians don't show respect for, or honestly serve, common tax-paying citizens needs a total overhaul in its political infrastructure. Politicians are sample representatives of the people. Unless people improve qualitatively and conscientiously, the quality of politics and politicians won't improve.

Indian Television Must Shift to Real Issues

While people and television channels in India keep busy discussing politicians and political parties, India keeps slipping further.

- India stealthily adds nearly 60,000 new people every day to its population, which exacerbates the already-high pressure on the resources in the country.
- About 50,000 new vehicles start using the roads every 24 hours, polluting the environment further, increasing the travel time and the travel fatigue; and exacerbating the loss of precious human time and human happiness.
- The air quality and the water quality keep deteriorating every minute.
- The country is getting hotter and the groundwater is depleting with each year.
- Kashmiri Pandits continue to be called migrants and live in exile, dispersed across India and overseas, far away from their native home.
- Many women—young and old—are being raped or killed every day, or are on the radar of potential rapists and killers.
- More people, especially the youth, army *jawans* and farmers are committing suicide every day, or are contemplating it, because they are unhappy.
- Millions of rupees are exchanging hands under (or over) the table every hour, as part of rampant ongoing corruption in all walks of daily life.

Indian people love to idolise politicians. In my childhood, they idolised Indira Gandhi. Before my birth, they idolised Mahatma Gandhi and Nehru. These days, they idolise many leaders. The term 'idolise' reflects 'love' and 'bhakti'. As they say, love is blind. Indian people's love for their leaders has taken away their sense of 'right' and 'wrong'. People justify the use of doctored messages and videos—as propaganda—as long as these potentially benefit their beloved leader. But wrong is wrong! Is it not? It used to be wrong, in the distant past! But, this is 2019, and now all is fair in love and war!

God save India. India will soon enjoy a consolatory win against China in terms of population. She may, however, never be able to beat that nation in many key areas—education, sports, overall wealth and global impact, science & technology, liveability & happiness, defence etc.

> *A country is defined by the values, conscientiousness, citizenship and discipline practically exhibited in daily life by its people.*

The Great Indian Democracy

What a mockery of democracy exists in India! The pressures of changing times, a constant battle to survive and a sickening political tug of war have made the common definitions of 'right' and 'wrong' very subjective. Sadly, the focus is not about doing the right, as defined universally; the focus is on grabbing power and then, shamelessly, showing it off boisterously. Politicians live in a world of their own, far remote from the common people whom they are meant to serve. Instead of servitude, they acquire unethical lordship over common people. Many proverbs become relevant in the context of Indian politics and the Indian election process:

- Money makes the mare go.
- Might is right.
- Show me the face and I'll show you the rules.
- Everything is fair in love and war.
- The end justifies the means.
- Grab power by hook or by crook.

Perhaps, the Indian politicians have forgotten the following time-proven wise sayings:

- Honesty is the best policy.
- Two wrongs do not make one right.
- What goes around comes around.
- Pride goes before a fall.
- What goes up comes down.
- Life goes in a circle.
- Time and tide wait for none.

- This too shall pass.
- Life is a great leveller.
- One eventually falls on one's own sword.
- Arrogance leads one to commit political suicide.
- One who digs a pit for others himself falls into it.

Elections are fought solely for power and not for serving the general population. It is mind boggling to see the amount of money that is allegedly being spent for buying the people's votes, then the seats and, finally, the elected lawmakers during horse-trading. No wonder, India remains a poor country, despite the many shopping malls and luxurious lifestyle of the neo-rich and the famous.

The common person in India goes about his daily business to survive and can't afford the time to fix the issues. Survival acquires a paramount importance. The media remains in business and mainly concerns itself with its rating. The social media remains abuzz with a comic excitement, but nothing substantial; lots of lies are being manufactured and doctored on purpose and spread on the social media to poison the community, cause social strife and malign the politicians and their parties. And the politicians very cleverly and quietly, and sometimes not so cleverly or quietly, rather foolishly, keep doing what they know best—divide and rule, gather wealth and consolidate power.

India needs active citizens and proactive citizenship, and not politicians or political parties.

National Character Building

The eminent panel members at my book launch at Chennai, on 17 November 2017, unequivocally agreed that India urgently needs a national character (re)building exercise—at all levels and in all communities. The question is how to do it, considering India is a multi-racial, multi-ethnic and multi-faith country. Religion, caste and ethnicity play a major part in people's general outlook and behaviour. The rest of the world sees the people living in India, and those coming out of the country, as 'Indians', but the people living in India don't see themselves first as Indians; they see themselves first as Hindus, Muslims, Sikhs … or Bengali, Bihari, Punjabi … or SC /ST, and even along the regional divide—north or south Indians.

The essential sense of belonging is seen to be missing in most people living in the country. Therefore, how and from where to start the seemingly uphill, rather impossible task of national 'character building'? A million dollar question is if this task is worth doing at all? Don't the wise and the intelligent in India keep a low profile, and go about their daily lives without causing any fuss or attracting attention to themselves? Are they not waiting for the chaos to sort itself out naturally?

Will writing books on the subject really help, considering most people are happy messaging their ego on social media and watching those television debates with interest? Books are not generally considered attractive or important, which also reflects a character of its own kind. How ironical it is that some communities, who claim to be literary and intelligent, don't generally buy and read books; they keep busy messaging on the social media and show a clear preference for dining out at expensive eating places, showing off their expensive clothing and jewellery, and hosting lavish social and wedding parties. Then how to build a national character?

He (JL Nehru) had no blueprint before him; he inherited a divided British India. Infrastructure projects were his temples. He tried to be 'too' good and statesmanlike, but being 'too' good is never good, it bites back. Indians were used to autocracy, aristocracy and dictatorial rules. Democracy was too much for them to digest. He did not read them well enough.

Nehru was a human being, but never a bad human being. Humans do err and some commit blunders. But no human is perfect. We were told Lord Ram was perfect—Purushottam. But many people criticise Him too on at least two controversial accounts—exiling Mother Sita and the execution of King Bali. That is the problem with humans—they make mistakes. They blunder at times. They are never perfect.

> *Governments are not honest or corrupt, individual people are; people form political parties and governments. Leaders can make a difference, but not always considering their team represents the same batch of mix. Unless people move towards honesty and care for the country, it does not matter which government rules.*

Stereotyping Communities is Wrong

In 1989-1990, it was wrong to stereotype the entire Kashmiri Pandit community in Kashmir as *Sanghis*, or the RSS workers, or the agents of India. Around 95 percent, or more Kashmiri Pandits were the supporters of the Congress or NC parties, or both. Both parties claimed to be secular and had Kashmiri connections. Pandits followed the Congress party because of Pt JL Nehru, who claimed to be a Kashmiri. It was logical that they also followed his daughter, Indira Gandhi, and then her son, Rajiv Gandhi.

It is also completely wrong to stereotype the entire Kashmiri Muslim community as radicalised and as a militant community. Like Pandits, more than 95 percent of the Kashmiri Muslim community has always been mainstream and tolerant, generally following spiritual Islam. Then why did they not oppose the armed militants in 1990 and stop Pandits from leaving? The answer is: 'The fear of the gun'.

How many of us can dare to speak if we know or suspect a gun is lurking somewhere in the vicinity? Who does not know that many Kashmiri Muslim fathers and brothers were killed by their own blood? Those were very dark days. Everyone was blinded. The gun was new to Kashmir. People did not know what to do. Who does not know that hundreds, perhaps thousands, of Kashmiri Muslims, serving in the police and Indian armed forces, have laid down their lives fighting the militants? Tearing apart the two communities is child's play but to stitch the two communities back requires honest people from both sides, with wisdom, vision, guts, sincerity, perseverance and dedication.

Stereotyping poisons our thoughts and outlook. We must correct our psychology with reason, logic and evidential facts.

They feel entitled to take the leadership of people—with an intent to lord over them—because the educated and much more intelligent individuals selfishly choose to look after their own careers and work as professionals. In the past, the best students would be chosen as class monitors and prefects. Just wondering if that still happens! If yes, where do these class monitors and prefects land in their careers? Shouldn't they all take political science and law streams to become lawmakers if India has to change for the better?

Unlike the western democracies, China has a different political structure. But, with mostly engineers at the helm, China has strongly emerged as a world superpower. The reason is that, like lawyers, engineers also follow a logical approach, based on reason and evidence. In western countries, generally (not always), the heads of the states and lawmakers, and most of the politicians, have law degrees. And to enter a law school, one must be brilliant and meritorious in studies. That is one reason that Western democracies are healthy and mostly based on reason and logic, and lies and deceit are less likely to be rewarded.

India has a great fleet of well-educated and experienced professionals—engineers, doctors, scientists, educators, lawyers and soldiers. Not many of them make their thoughts known. Is it because they are constantly busy with running the country, while others just talk and take credit for their hard work.

I have lost a number of my close friends and relatives for my neutral socio-political views and a constant rant against the current population and dwindling liveability issues. One day they will look for me and say I was correct in my assessments. Hope it is not too late by then. People have labelled me differently at various times. Some say I am in love with this or that community. Some say I don't know India well enough, so I must first live there. Some exhort me to join the mainstream politics. I am doing what I know best—keep raising awareness.

If you really love and care for your country, then work at least

India needs a leader who does not work for any organisation or any political party alone; a leader who works for the country as a whole and all the people—Indian people—and not individually for Hindus or Muslims or Christians or Sikhs or Dalits. Unless India has such an autonomous visionary and dynamic leader, it has no hope. How frightening it is to imagine India in 2025—a Hindu Rashtra, sans minorities and the Congress party, but volatile and restless—Dalits fighting the upper caste Hindus—Brahmins fighting Thakurs–the south fighting the north—east fighting the west –the poor fighting the rich and hunger—farmers fighting drought, floods and suicide—youth fighting joblessness, mental anxiety and depression—and all fighting climate change, lung diseases, TB and cancers!

When people lose faith in law & order, they become vigilantes. The civilian chowkidars in India have also lost faith in the army and the internal law & order. However, instead of carrying bamboo sticks and patrolling through the streets of India, they waste their time on social media? India can't afford any more internal strife. India has one of the largest and a very formidable/elite defence force. It also has a very large internal security force. Then why do civilians need to be chowkidars? Do they doubt the jawans? Is that not insulting to the security personnel?

Unless a leader turns into a caring and nurturing mother, he/she ain't a complete leader. A mother does not differentiate, she feeds all. Dogs have been known to breastfeed human babies and lion cubs. Hail the mother! Politics and political euphoria drug people. They become blissfully oblivious of their existential threats. Instead of looking after their country, they play to the tunes of their Pied Pipers.

A good leader needs just one valid reason to solve a problem but a politician comes up with a thousand reasons not to solve it.

Has anyone tried to imagine how India 2019 would have looked without MK Gandhi and JL Nehru of 1947? Before answering, let us read the history of British India. Let us prove all negative, divisive forces wrong and together defeat them.

In a matured and healthy democracy, the contesting political parties publicly list the set of national issues, and discuss how they intend to address them. But, in India, it is street politics. Politicians mainly indulge in mudslinging. When a community loses its hope, vision and wisdom, and follows like a herd, nothing can save it from itself. A simple, honest and straight approach disarms devious minds; it makes them defenceless and angry. They explode and lose. Creating and feeding religious divides is a proven political trump card. Sadly, it works, as people get emotionally driven. Pakistan (an Islamic country) and Nepal (a Hindu country) are examples why Asian countries haven't made much progress despite having a national religion.

Regionalism, casteism, feudalism, racialism, cronyism, nepotism and corruption would still plague the Indian community even if India were to become a 100-percent Hindu Rashtra. Raising religious issues is a deliberate political distraction from real, deeper issues of power politics and people's poverty.

The more I travel around our planet, the more I see my own reflection in other humans of different lands—from different cultures, creed, colours, languages etc. No cultural shocks for me in our lovely global village.

For integrity and political health, India must call a referendum ASAP about the introduction of the American two-party system of democracy, with a Presidential form of government. The current Westminster form is paralysing even the British parliament; just look at the BREXIT stalemate. India follows a multi-party system and a Westminster form of government, which is showing its serious flaws. Look at the UK itself. For better governance, India should follow the US, the older democracy, and adopt a 2-party system, with a Presidential form of government. Alternatively, due to a comparable high population, India may follow the Chinese system. In any case, the current system is an unnecessary waste of time and opportunity for Indians.

Australia and India follow the Westminster form of governance. Due to a much smaller population, an Australian vote is nearly 55 times stronger than an Indian vote. Plus every Australian voter is

- 2,150 deaths due to cancer
- 600 deaths due to tuberculosis
- 400 deaths due to road accidents
- 370 deaths due to suicides
- 140 rapes
- 60 deaths due to murders and homicide
- 25 deaths due to rape
- Ten (10) deaths due to potholes on roads
- Two (2) deaths (actually 1.65) due to terrorism related incidents

While security forces fight terrorists, civilians must make some noise for preventing those 3,500 deaths and 140 rapes every day. Sadly, I don't think they really care, because it is not jingoism.

> *Many people wish and call for an open full war between India and Pakistan. Both armies lost a total of up to or around 40 thousand soldiers in the previous four wars. How many more are we prepared to lose now? Our call may be called legitimate only if we and our children are expected to be fighting on the front; if not, we must just shut up.*

The Great Indian Political Circus

One must love India for its vibrant, free-for-all democracy. India may fall in the 'flawed' category on Democracy Index, and still keep falling, but on the other hand, it is also truly unmatched in its high entertainment value.

The great Indian democracy is quite unique in so many ways. No wonder Indians claim '*Sare jahan se achha Hindustan hamara*'. Anyone can be a lawmaker in India—virtually anyone—and anyone can say anything against anyone or anything, without any iota of responsibility or accountability. People just don't care. Such freedom of speech and action is astoundingly unparalleled.

Politics is one of the leading professions in India. One does not need to be educated or civil to be a politician. The great Indian political industry has learnt and mastered the fine tricks of (mock) fighting of WWF wrestling and the cinema. Public loves to see politicians fighting, same way as they also love the hero fighting the villain in a movie.

'If rape is inevitable, sit back and enjoy being raped', such goes a wise advice. You may then have some chance of saving your life, but without any guarantee. There is a real chance that you may get raped and still be finished. If you are thick-skinned and not slavishly aligned to any political party or any politician, or not obsessed with morality, ethics, values, decency or virtues, there is never a dull moment for you. There is no better place than India to watch a multi-dimensional 24 x 7 live political circus, with such immense entertainment value, on television, social media, public speeches and media interviews. Those evening political debates on television, where all debaters speak at the same time and the audience can hardly hear anything, defy common sense and logic.

Don't expect Indian politics to change anytime soon, as Indians love it the way it is. It is not a matter of intelligence; it is just another version of WWF and cinema fighting. Save your mental energy for helping yourself. Politics is a brutal power game, played mercilessly by influential actors who use the public as pawns and exploit their emotions; it is not for the fainthearted or the thin-skinned.

Indian and Pakistani Armies are Not Fools

Indian and Pakistani militaries are not lunatics. Some interesting 20th century war statistics:

- World War I (For 4 Years, from 28 July 1914 to 11 November 1918)—total 15 to 19 million deaths
- World War II (1 Sept 1939 to 14 April 1945)—total 70 to 85 million deaths, including 50 to 55 million civilian deaths
- Vietnam War (For 20 years, from 1 Nov 1955 to 30 April 1975)—total 1.33 to 4.35 million deaths, including 58,318 US troops
- Iran-Iraq War (For 8 years, from 22 Sept 1980 to 20 Aug

1988)—total 1.25 to 1.50 million deaths

- Gulf War 1 (For 6 months, from 21 Aug 1990 to 28 Feb 1991)—from 25,000 to 50,000 deaths
- Iraq War (For 8 years and 8 months, from 20 March 2003 to 18 Dec 2011), from 151,000 to 461, 000 deaths

In comparison to the above, the total cumulative death toll from all four Indo-Pak wars since 1946 is estimated to be in the order of 30,000 to 40,000. One can reasonably conclude Indians and Pakistanis are not as deadly towards each other as others.

This may not be good news for warmongers on both sides. They must understand that Indians and Pakistanis are not lunatics like others; therefore, they will avoid major wars in the future too. They have learnt that no one really wins a war. Every war creates deep generational destruction, which future generations from both sides inherit and pay the price for.

The Westminster system of governance has for quite some time been showing its downside and shortfalls (which could, however, be perceived by some as hallmarks) in the UK and India, as well as here in Australia. Nothing you do as the Government will be judged as acceptable by the Opposition. They will try everything to shred to pieces what you propose. At times, they go to the extent of throwing their kitchen sink to sink the Government.

How unfortunate is it for any country where the Opposition solely dedicates itself to undermine the Government and attacks everything that the Government says or does, till the system stalls and the Government falls! Sadly, many good initiatives proposed by Government slip through the cracks. As a direct result, the country suffers and people lose. It is time for people to reassess the suitability of the Westminster system and then come up with a right system of governance.

India has introduced several documents to prove one's identity—Identity card, Passport (if one has it), Voter card, Ration Card, Aadhaar Card, Pension Card, PAN card etc. Strangely though, India has not yet introduced a DNA Card to prove one is actually a biological child of one's known father, and not the neighbour's. The father-child relationship seems to be based mainly on faith and trust. Not many children ask their father to provide valid evidence that he is their biological father. Where has the trust-factor disappeared? Who undermined it? Why is there so much fear in the country? India was not always like this! Where is India heading to?

The world is increasingly becoming more evidence-based, as it logically should be. Nothing is or should be taken at the face value. It is not uncommon these days to consult several doctors to take a second or a third or even a fourth opinion, just to make sure. It does not matter what you believe, what matters is if you are able to produce evidence or a valid proof to support your belief or a claim. Is it the time for DNA cards? A DNA Card could definitely be used to settle family disputes—family inheritance and divorce cases. As such, it could be used to prove if you are truly eligible to inherit the wealth and property of a man whom you claim to be your father. Secondly, it could support a father's will in favour of the people who claim to be his children. How far can we go? Will all belief systems eventually go? Interesting times, the world is changing.

> *Patriotism also means having to establish friendly and cordial relationship with all your neighbouring countries so that all people live in peace. Patriotism does not mean jingoism.*

Lessons from the Mahabharata and Bhagwad Gita

Your loyalty must be first to your country, then the king, and not the other way round. Always be on the side of dharma (righteousness).

Always keep your eyes open. Never be a passive witness to wrong actions done by the people around you. Act without any expectation of rewards in return. Your true self is your soul, which is indestructible.

Open Letter to Mr Imran Khan, the PM of Pakistan

"Mr Imran Khan, almost 27 years ago, on 25 March 1992, you made history at the MCG when you lifted the ODI World Cup. How you

> *Leaders are very few, most are followers. Not many can think independently. One needs strong and independent convictions and vision to lead and stand proud.*

India and Pakistan Must Work Together

India and Pakistan, instead of fighting against each other, must join hands to fight terrorism on their soils. Both countries have been suffering. The two neighbours can't abandon each other. They were born from the same country—British India. They have to learn to coexist peacefully in each other's close proximity. One would wish, together as good neighbours, they fight significant human issues that seriously affect their countries—poverty, illiteracy and poor education, gender issues, and the negative effects of climate change.

It will be a much better world when Indian and Pakistani professionals (teachers, engineers, doctors etc.) work in each other's countries, and the armies of the two countries conduct joint war exercises to fight common wars. Can the two neighbours learn from Australia and New Zealand how to coexist peacefully as close and friendly neighbours; or from the US and Canada; or from the European countries?

The selfish and unwise perpetrators of violence in Kashmir (and elsewhere) repeatedly forget that violence is no solution to address any issue. They don't learn anything from history, they simply forget that violence begets nothing but hate and violence as reaction from the other side and, in the end, achieves nothing but their own self-destruction. Their selfishness blinds them to prudence and pragmatism.

Terrorists are the real enemies of the Kashmiri people. They are bent upon completely destabilising and destroying Kashmir. They want to turn Kashmir into Afghanistan or like any other unstable, volatile country in the Middle East or Africa, where peace has been absent for decades. They want to destroy the lives of millions of Kashmiris. Had they been wise and caring for their people, they would have strived for a peaceful resolution of the issue, if at all any. The onus is well and truly on the common Kashmiri people to check, report and handover the terrorists to the authorities so that peace and normalcy can return quickly to the valley. All political and social issues can be addressed peacefully by consistent, well-intentioned dialogue and negotiations.

In order to solve a problem, one must first understand and accept the cause of the problem. Problems must not be brushed under the carpet; they must be faced and tackled head-on, with a genuine intent and action to address them. The ostrich attitude has never helped anyone. The bull must be held by its horns. Problems don't solve all by themselves. Waiting games never pay off.

Half-hearted and half-baked solutions only exacerbate the problems. The misuse or under-dose of an antibiotic makes the bug resistant to the drug. Crying alone does not help actions matter. Offering lip sympathies is a fashion in this day and age of materialism. Who has lost sleep? Has anyone fasted? Has anyone visited the scene of the crime? Has anyone visited the aggrieved family of a victim? Leaders don't Tweet condemnations, they act first and then Tweet, announcing that an appropriate action has been already undertaken. Tweeting alone—without first taking an immediate punitive and preventive action—has the potential to embolden the aggressor. How many times will the same condemnation be repeated? What is new in it? The Tweeted message loses its effect as it is repeated over and over again after repeat incidents. A serious introspection is necessary to prevent recurrences of a misadventure. Why did it happen? Can it happen again? What will prevent it from any recurrence?

India's Political Gain May Be Kashmiri Pandits' Permanent Loss of Home

Abrogation of Article 370 of the Indian Constitution, on 5 August 2019, may seem to be the current Indian government's political win, at least in the short term. The actual long-term picture will possibly take quite some time to emerge, in particular, when the additional security forces—rushed to the valley in the first week of August 2019—

are withdrawn. On the basis of the political history of Kashmir—both before and after 1947—and that of the wider region, it will not be unreasonable to expect that a severe local, and possibly regional, backlash may potentially be in the offing against the abrogation of Article 370. The overall picture in the valley appears to be hazy at the moment and subject to a range of speculations—dangling between some wishful optimism and a more realistic pessimism, as the valley is known to be currently experiencing strict restrictions on the general movement of people and their communication via internet and mobile phones. At this stage, therefore, one can't be carried away in making any definitive conclusions about the future of Kashmir, howsoever tempting or exciting that may seem to be.

Regardless of what happens in Kashmir from hereafter, Kashmiri Pandits may have now possibly lost Kashmir, perhaps forever. Kashmiri Muslims may never forgive them or accept them back. Kashmiri Muslims may draw parallels between the exodus of Pandits from their home in 1990 and the recent evacuation of Hindu pilgrims from the annual Amarnath Yatra and the Indian students from National Institute of Technology, Srinagar, during the days leading to the abrogation of Article 370. In general, Kashmiri Muslims have always maintained that the exodus of Kashmiri Pandits in 1990 was triggered and facilitated by the Indian government, a claim that has historically been outrightly rejected by Kashmiri Pandits. The Indian electronic media has also shown some Kashmiri Pandits celebrating and rejoicing on learning about the abrogation, which may not sit well with the majority Muslim population in the valley.

As far as the return of Kashmiri Pandits is concerned, that can only happen when the majority Muslim population greets and receives them warmly, from the heart. But hearts can never be stitched back by force. Pandits can never be pushed back to the valley in the same manner as hundreds of thousands of Indian troops have been pushed into the valley over the last three decades. To cohere and thrive in Kashmir, Pandits undoubtedly need warm hugs and expressed acceptance of goodwill, with a warm hand of friendship from their Kashmiri Muslim brethren.

As before, it appears, therefore, Kashmiri Pandits may have been made a sacrificial community, a collateral casualty of India's recent abrupt action via-a-via Kashmir, which appears to have been done to fulfil the generational ambitions of millions of Indians to own properties in Kashmir. If Kashmiri Pandits had not existed in Kashmir until 1990, despite being only about 4 to 5 percent of the population in Kashmir, India could not have held on—morally, politically or otherwise—to a 100-percent Muslim populated valley, based on the principles of the partition of British India, particularly if Kashmiri Muslim populace did not want to live with India.

India and Indians owe Kashmiri Pandits a great debt for their historical sacrifices—pre and post 1947 and, thereafter, in 1990 and 2019. India's win may possibly prove to be Pandits' permanent loss.

Breaking is easy, burning is easy, crushing is easy, cutting is easy, destroying is easy, ripping is easy. Anyone can do these things, even children. It does not take much time to do them. An acid tongue and a poison pen too can do them with great ease. Building is difficult, creating is difficult, grafting is difficult; joining is difficult, preserving is difficult, stitching is difficult. Not everyone can do these things. Healing wounds—mental and physical—and stitching back communities needs vision, wisdom, forbearance, love, empathy, compassion, kindness, benevolence and patience, which one receives only by Divine Grace. Those who heal—using care, kindness, empathy and compassion—live forever.

War

Most people, if not all, fear war, death and destruction. Why? Because most people live with the fear of the unknown! Some also fear the night, for fear of darkness and the dark forces that they imagine lurk and attack under the veil of darkness. They wait nervously to see the sunrise. Some also fear the murky winter, for fear of the cold and gloom. They crave for the arrival of the spring—the life, with all its glory, warmth and colours. They know what they fear is transitory and not much of an unknown. They also learn their unique ways to manage their fears and how to bide time through difficult periods.

Regardless of whether or not one fears war and death, both are unavoidable, as nightfall is inevitable after sunset and winter after autumn. To alleviate such fears, albeit to a limited extent, religions introduced the concepts of heaven and hell, and reincarnation, encouraging humans to indulge only in good and righteous actions, but leaving ample room for the subjectiveness of the terms 'good' and 'righteousness', which has led to severe discord amongst humans since the times immemorial.

Apparently, on the surface, some people do seem to believe in the concepts of heaven and hell, and reincarnation, but deep down most, if not all, fear death due to the fear of the unknown. Believing is one thing and knowing is another thing. The ground reality is no one knows what really happens after one dies. Thus, it will be useful if one talks about the subject matter in a more philosophical language.

Is War Good or Bad?

As such, there is nothing good or bad about war, as there is nothing good or bad about death. That is the way they are. Whilst death is natural, and must be accepted, war is a direct result of the human nature—boredom, greed and territorial ambitions, power and control, revenge, self-aggrandisement and self-immortalisation of the warring leaders, and their necessity to remain in power and fuel their country's economy.

It is true that humans don't realise the value of the day unless they see the night. The value of good health is realised only when one falls sick and becomes diseased or disabled. The value of that little finger is realised only after one loses it. Similarly, the value of peace and life is realised only after one goes through war and destruction. It is Nature's way to remind humans what peace means and Nature works also through humans. But humans get bored with peace and start flirting with the dangers of war.

Nature designs its onslaught with such subtlety that even the best of men—educated and intelligent—become blinded to irreversible, bloody consequences of their belligerent actions. But Nature never gets blamed; Hitler and Mussolini are demonised forever. People forget these leaders had enjoyed a great mass following. Directly or indirectly, their followers contributed equally in making them dictators and exhorted them to do what they eventually did to appease their masses—all for clinging to power though. These leaders hardly carried any firearms but their charisma was just enough to make them the spearhead of their masses. The ground reality, however, was that these leaders were just figureheads. The base of their power and ideologies rested with their faceless masses and followers. It is ironical that people create their own gods of doom and destruction; they worship them through their unquestionable slavish servitude.

If there was eternal peace on the planet, one would call it a heaven, but a boring heaven. If all people on the earth were happy and materially satisfied all the time, it would be a dull and boring place; and the human world would not be able to sustain itself from an economic point of view. Imagine yourself eating your choicest dessert all the time; you will go crazy after a few days. Have you ever figured out why young people pay hundreds of dollars for purchasing just a branded, faded and shredded, pair of jeans?

Let us learn from Nature. The way we accept death, first philosophically and finally physically—as soon as we discover there is no other way out—we are left with no other option but also to accept war. It is the way it is and it will always be as it has been. When was the world peaceful? It has been only 101 years and 74 years, respectively, since World Wars I and II ended. In the last seven decades, how many decades did not see a major military conflict on the planet?

War—A Part of Life?

War doesn't happen just like that—out of the blue and for no reason; it is planned, crafted and engineered to serve the political, strategic economic interests and ambitions of faceless powers.

A famous Sanskrit proverb warns: '*vinaash kale vipreet buddhi*', which means when one's fall is imminent, one loses wisdom. Most wars are undoubtedly unnecessary and triggered for trivial, jingoistic and political reasons.

Some wars are thrust upon other nations who find it necessary to fight them for their existential reasons. When a country faces a number of significant internal challenges, most of which may be its own creations, and suddenly faces the prospect of imploding, as a direct result of a sudden threat on its borders, it is left to choose between only two options—do nothing or fight the external threat. The latter option gives it a slim chance to survive and retain its integrity. If it chooses to do nothing to address the external threat, it can survive and remain integrated only if it is able to successfully address all its internal issues, which may be more of an uphill battle, possibly impossible to be won. Countries, like humans, invariably take the path of least resistance.

Shrouded within all its enigmatic, dark mysteriousness, the slope of war can be so steep and slippery that, even before you realise, you are already fighting it as soon as you start flirting with it. On the one end of the power spectrum, it intoxicates the most intelligent and the powerful, and on the other, it petrifies and numbs those who are under threat. One thing leads to the other till hell suddenly breaks loose and things spiral downwards beyond anyone's control. All one thinks about is how to maximise the kill on the other side, or how to minimise the losses on your side.

At the end of the devastation, even though a country may claim victory, the truth is no one actually wins a war. Humanity loses in all cases. On all sides, humans suffer, bleed, die and become scarred and disabled forever—both mentally and physically. There is no glory in war; there is no glory in killing and destroying. War is sheer madness irrespective of who starts it and how it ends.

Indian epics, Ramayana and Mahabharata, provide ample warning against war but when did the Indian subcontinent ever see any century without war? Man has never learnt to live peacefully and never shall; ambitions, revenge and greed have always got the better of him. Perhaps also because the Bhagwad Gita declares one's soul is indestructible and one must fight for the *dharma*. However, the meaning of the term *dharma* has been subject to varied interpretations of time and place, as also religion. What may appear as *dharma* to one may appear as *adharma* to another person; man knows how to justify the means to achieve the intended end.

Can War Be Avoided?

War can be avoided but only if rigidity gives way to flexibility; short-term selfishness gives way to long-term benevolence; jingoism gives way to globalism; politics-driven nationalism gives way to responsible patriotism; and greed gives in to wisdom; and above all, if common sense is allowed to prevail.

It is prudent never to start a war if you don't know how to finish it. In many cases, the actual ground scenario may prove your challenges are much bigger that you had expected and your perceived enemy is a much tougher adversary than you anticipated. You may realise you may have bitten off more than you could chew.

War can be avoided if leaders surround themselves with true friends, with conscience and not by sycophants; those who don't appease them for fear of displeasure and reprisal, those who provide them with honest advice, without political correctness, howsoever, bitter that advice may be. Men of conscience speak the truth and out of wisdom.

War can be avoided if leaders follow their conscience. Sadly, conscience remains buried under ego and pride.

War can't be avoided if salvageable situations are not addressed wisely by making simple, timely, face-saving U-turns—only for the greater good of mankind—but instead are facilitated to deteriorate and worsen, and allowed to turn into pressure-cookers, based on wrong assumptions of one or both warring parties.

What after the Final War?

Nature destroys what is created before recreating it again. As old leaves fall in autumn and trees suffer naked in the cold of winter, new leaves appear in spring and trees bask again in the summer sun. Man is a strange work of Nature and, thus, Nature also works through man. It is in the man's nature to destroy what is created and reconstruct what is destroyed. Destruction is essential before reconstruction commences.

Let us learn from Nature and derive a hope that the human race will get wiped out. This planet will see new civilisations in the future as the present ones will gradually fade or even disappear suddenly into oblivion. New people will arrive and traverse the earth despite our continued endeavour—in the name of our progress—to create and pile up all possible means of our own destruction. As long as there is one healthy woman and one healthy man left on the earth to cohabit and copulate, the human race will continue. And then, new religions will be born, which will divide humans. New means and methods of destruction will also be created. The cycles of creation and destruction will continue perpetually till the sun shines.

But what if the human race is completely wiped out? What happens after the sun expands and devours all the planets in the solar system in the end? Nothing will return to nothing; it will be dark and silent again or perhaps not.

The human creation and evolution have done no great favours to our planet, perhaps their complete destruction may. Humans multiplied their population more than seven times in the last four centuries—thanks to the dawn of the Industrial Age and the subsequent advancement in various sciences and technologies. Their multiplication exacerbated their insatiable hunger for power and energy, which undermined their very existence. They disturbed Nature; they must pay for their misdeeds.

Now what does this argument lead to? It inspires us to recognise the transitory nature of life and, therefore, a need to live every moment that we are left with. Let us live till we have the opportunity to do so. Let us accept the rewards of our actions—*karma*. We deserve every bit of what has happened to us in the past and equally what will happen to us in the future. We created our destiny, there is no escape.

A pressure cooker explodes like a bomb if it is not removed from heat in a timely manner, especially when its pressure-valve is sealed and not allowed to vent out the internal pressure build-up. A retention wall collapses suddenly, with disastrous consequences, if it is loaded mindlessly beyond its capacity during a heavy rainfall, especially if its weepholes are plugged. Water on the hills must be provided with adequate flow-path or it can silently seep into the ground and build immense pressure, which can trigger an avalanche that destroys everything in its path.

> *A victory that does not bring in genuine peace and happiness for both the victor and the vanquished is not truly a victory; it is a new seed for the next stage of a conflict, potentially much bigger and with much more hate, vengeance and retribution. The victory that is achieved by genuinely winning hearts and sincerely addressing the core issues, and not by using force in any shape or form, brings in sustainable peace.*

Our Current Fragile World

Such an alarmingly high degree of socio-political polarisation across the world—especially in the militarily powerful, major economies—looks unprecedented, at least since the end of World War II. It looks scarily very black and white, with only a narrow band of grey in between. People either absolutely adore the current world leaders or hate them absolutely, without much confusion in announcing their feelings. The looming battle lines seem to be drawn at all levels; it may only be a matter of time before all hell breaks loose. Such stark polarisation reflects an ominous sign of the times to come—an extremely fragile world order, with individuals standing against individuals from the same communities; communities against communities; ethnicities against ethnicities; and countries against countries.

Humans are fast priming themselves, or rather being manipulated and tricked, to fight one another—with anything imaginable they can readily find to fight—social and mass media, sticks, stones, swords,